ANTICIPATING THE END TIMES

Anticipating the End Times

A Concise Commentary

on

The Book of Daniel

Malcolm C. Davis

JOHN RITCHIE LTD
CHRISTIAN PUBLICATIONS

40 Beansburn, Kilmarnock, Scotland

ISBN-13: 978 1 907731 02 0

Copyright © 2010 by John Ritchie Ltd.
40 Beansburn, Kilmarnock, Scotland

www.ritchiechristianmedia.co.uk

Typeset by John Ritchie Ltd., Kilmarnock
Printed by Bell & Bain Ltd., Glasgow

Dedication

*To the memory of my late parents, Mr and Mrs F. Cyril Davis,
who first instructed me in the teaching of the Scriptures.*

Acknowledgements

I wish to thank the following people for their respective roles in the publication of this book: Mr Edwin Taylor of Aberdeen for editing the whole manuscript helpfully; Mr John Riddle of Cheshunt for writing the Foreword; the Wednesday afternoon Bible study group in Leeds for encouraging me in the writing of the book; and Mr Alan Cameron and the staff at John Ritchie Ltd for publishing the manuscript efficiently.

Leeds, June 2010

Contents

Foreword 9

Introduction 11

Chapter 1: The Making of a Man of God 22

Chapter 2: God's Panoramic Revelation of Future
            World History 29

Chapter 3: Faith's Fiery Trial 44

Chapter 4: The Great King's Humiliation and Testimony 51

Chapter 5: Weighed in God's Balances and Found Wanting 57

Chapter 6: Daniel's Deliverance from the Lions' Den 66

Chapter 7: God's View of the Five Future World Kingdoms 72

Chapter 8: The Vision of the Ram, the He Goat, and the
            King of Fierce Countenance 83

Chapter 9: Daniel's Prayer and God's Prophecy of
            Israel's Seventy Weeks Discipline 94

Chapter 10: Daniel's Final Vision of the Lord and the
            Revelation of Angelic Warfare 107

Chapter 11: The Vision continued with the Prediction of the
            Wars of the Kings of the North and South 113

Chapter 12: Understanding the End Times of Great Tribulation,
            Resurrection, and Millennial Blessing 130

Chapter 13: Daniel's Spiritual Legacy for Believers Today 142

Foreword

The Book of Daniel has engaged the minds of diverse groups of people, ranging from children in Sunday School, to erudite theologians. The account of Daniel's three friends in Nebuchadnezzar's "burning fiery furnace" together with the account of Daniel himself in "the den of lions", have filled many a child with wonder as the stories have been recounted to them, and other parts of the Book have filled many older people with perplexity as they have endeavoured to elucidate the meaning of the text! It must be said, however, that diligent and careful study of the Book of Daniel has always been amply rewarded, and that the promise made by the apostle Paul resonates well in the mouth of the prophet himself: "Consider what I say; for the Lord *shall* give thee understanding in all things" (2 Tim 2.7, RV).

Following the publication in 2009 of his helpful book *The Climax of World History*, rightly described as 'A concise study of the Revelation of Jesus Christ', Malcolm Davis has placed us further in his debt with the publication of *Anticipating the End Times*, 'A concise commentary on the Book of Daniel'. Those who read this book will not exclaim "much study is a weariness of the flesh"! The description, 'a concise commentary', is merited. The book is both concise and clear. In this respect, the author joins that noble band of Levites who "read in the book in the law of God distinctly, and gave the sense, and caused them to understand the reading" (Neh 8.8). He carefully establishes the meaning and significance of each chapter, always bearing in mind that after terrifying end-time conditions, preceded by the centuries-long course of four great world-empires, "the God of heaven" will "set up a kingdom which shall never be destroyed" (Dan 2.44). It will be – it must be – a literal kingdom.

It is always refreshing to read an exposition which clearly settles the meaning of a passage, rather than presenting a range of options, although this is necessary in some instances. In this connection, it is observable that where divergent views are held, Malcolm Davis is noticeably free from arrogance, without for one moment compromising with such errors as amillennialism. It should also be said that the exposition is punctuated with practical lessons. This is manifestly scriptural since, in the words of the apostle Peter, having spoken of future events, "what manner of persons ought ye to be in all holy conversation and godliness...?" (2 Pet 3.11).

I unhesitatingly commend *Anticipating the End Times*, trusting and praying that it will prove of lasting benefit to the Lord's people.

John Riddle
Cheshunt, Hertfordshire
June 2010

Introduction

The following concise commentary was originally prepared for the benefit of a small group of believers in our Lord Jesus Christ who met to study the Book of Daniel during a period of some months in 2009/10. Its aim is to explain the main message of the book, and to highlight major themes within it, so that readers who are unable to digest a very detailed and lengthy commentary can grasp its general characteristics and apply its lessons to their lives. The commentary includes some exegesis of the text and indications of the practical relevance of the book for believers today. A number of commentaries written by conservative and scholarly believers holding to the Premillennial interpretation of Scripture were consulted during the preparation of the work, which has benefited greatly from their use. The main principle followed in the interpretation of Daniel has been 'interpret literally wherever possible', and obviously symbolical passages have been understood to refer to actual people, objects, and events, not just vague abstract ideas. This study is issued in book form with the prayer that it may help fellow-believers to understand this vital Old Testament prophetic book better than they have until now, and to come to trust and love the great God of heaven who originally inspired its writing through His greatly-beloved servant Daniel. There are many indications in the world around us that the end times of which he speaks will probably come upon mankind soon. So, may we all learn to live in the light and good of its histories and prophecies until the Lord Jesus comes again for us!

Concerning The Book Of Daniel

1. Its Unique Character

The Book of Daniel is remarkable in two main ways. First of all, it is an inspiring autobiography of the man Daniel himself, a captive from Judah who became a prominent statesman in the administration of two Gentile world empires, but never lost either his faith or his character as a godly servant of the Lord his God. Secondly, it contains some of the most far-reaching and revealing prophecies concerning the future of world history, and the Jewish nation in particular, in the whole of the Bible. It is the indispensable background to many New Testament prophecies, and the Book of Revelation in particular.

2. The Significance of its Canonical Position within Scripture

In our Bibles the Book of Daniel is placed as the last, and latest, of the Major Prophetical Books, since it claims to have been written during Daniel's lifetime in the sixth century B.C., while the Jews were in exile in Babylon. In the Hebrew Bible, however, it is not placed amongst the Latter Prophets, but in the third major division of the Jews' Bible, the Writings. This may be because Daniel was first and foremost a statesman, rather than a prophet, although he certainly had the gift of prophecy. However, the positioning of the book by the Holy Spirit within the usual Christian canon is significant and full of spiritual meaning. The Major Prophets Isaiah, Jeremiah (plus Lamentations as a kind of appendix to his book), and Ezekiel all precede Daniel, which is thus the fourth main section of the Prophetical books. The twelve Minor Prophets follow it as the fifth and final section. Now it is possible to observe a harmonising thought pattern and structure in the Prophetical books with the first five books of our Bible. Isaiah corresponds to Genesis, Jeremiah plus Lamentations corresponds to Exodus, Ezekiel corresponds to Leviticus, and Daniel corresponds to Numbers, while the twelve Minor Prophets correspond to Deuteronomy, reiterating and reinforcing the instruction of the previous books. A little thought and study will reveal significant links between these Prophetical books and the books of the Pentateuch.

Certainly, with reference to the Book of Daniel, the 'Numbers' character of the book is quite evident to the thoughtful reader. In Daniel Israel is seen in the midst of the Gentile nations for their sins, just as in Numbers Israel is seen wandering in the wilderness for their unbelief, outside the Promised Land. Numbers portrays Israel under trial and God's discipline, and records their failure in those circumstances. Daniel portrays Israel again under God's discipline for their sins, and that discipline is predicted to continue for many hundreds of years to come, even beyond our own day. In Numbers amidst the general apostasy there are a few faithful over-comers who fully trust the Lord, amongst whom are Joshua and Caleb. They alone of their generation were permitted to enter the Promised Land. In Daniel amidst the general apostasy of the exiled Jews Daniel and his three friends, Hananiah, Mishael, and Azariah, stand out from the crowd as faithful witnesses for their God. They form a believing remnant whom God uses to influence heathen emperors and predict the course of world and Jewish history for millennia to come.

3. Its Spiritual Purpose
As to the spiritual purpose of the book, two aspects should be considered. Firstly, the Book of Daniel, whose author's name significantly means 'God is my Judge', demonstrates convincingly the absolute sovereignty of the one true God in world history as a whole, and over the idol gods of the then-known world in particular. The book predicts that all history is predetermined by God's design and brought to pass by the princes of the nations and the good and evil angels, who influence those national rulers as God's agents. He overrules all their evil for ultimate good. Secondly, the book demonstrates that God's purposes of grace and love in His election of Israel as His chosen earthly people will eventually be fulfilled through their promised Messiah, despite their rejection of Him,

consequent domination by the Gentile nations, and their dispersion amongst the nations for many years. He is still His failing people Israel's Lord God in spite of all they have done. The book of Daniel embraces the beginning, course, and end of the so-called 'Times of the Gentiles', during which period Israel will always be subject to God's discipline under the respective Gentile world kingdoms. The Book of Daniel opens with a reference to the first year of the Times of the Gentiles, which was 605 B.C., when Nebuchadnezzar first conquered Jerusalem and carried away Daniel and his three friends with many others to Babylon. These times will end at the 'time of the end' mentioned in Daniel chapter 12, when Christ comes again to reign over the whole world.

4. Its Wide Scope

The scope of the history and prophecies contained in this book is thus very wide and far-reaching. It extends from the beginning of the Babylonian exile, through their restoration to the land under Zerubbabel, Ezra, and Nehemiah, the later history of the Inter-Testamental period, the first coming of Christ with His rejection and crucifixion, the subsequent destruction of Jerusalem in A.D. 70, the present worldwide Dispersion of the Jews, and the detailed events of the future Great Tribulation, to the deliverance of the nation at the second coming of Christ to reign. It even includes a reference to the resurrection of the Old Testament saints to share in that rule. As in other Old Testament Scriptures, the book contains no reference to the Church, or the present age of God's grace in Christ. At certain points in the predictions there is an implied 'gap', which only New Testament revelation has later explained.

5. Its Use of the Names of God

The predominant names for God in the Book of Daniel are 'the God of heaven', 'the Most High', and 'the (sovereign) Lord', all of which are appropriate in a book which emphasises the Gentiles and the overruling sovereignty of God. Israel has been removed from their land and God's glory has departed from the Temple, which is now destroyed. Interestingly, the covenant name Jehovah (LORD) occurs only seven times in the book, and then only in chapter 9. Here Daniel in his classic prayer of confession and repentance on behalf of his sinful people Israel pleads the mercy of their covenant LORD God as the only basis of their restoration to the land of Israel at the end of the predetermined exile of seventy years in Babylon.

6. Its Portrayal of Daniel Himself

Daniel himself dominates most of the narrative and prophecies of the book. His exemplary wisdom and righteousness had become proverbial even in his own lifetime. His righteousness is referred to in Ezekiel chapter 14 verses 14 and 20, and his wisdom in Ezekiel chapter 28 verse 3. Ezekiel was a contemporary captive prophet in Babylonia. Daniel appears to have been the leader of the four faithful captive Jews in their stand for God, and certainly the most favoured of them all. He is called a 'man greatly-beloved' by God three times in the book itself; see chapter 9.23, 10.11 and 19. This favour was proved by the abundance of the revelations he received from his God. Truly, 'the secret of the Lord is with them that fear Him'. His life is exemplary and blameless in the recorded narratives, although he confessed his people's sins as his own, and undoubtedly felt the weight of them in his own soul. He was a foremost statesman under both Nebuchadnezzar and Darius, and 'continued until the first year of Cyrus', 538 B.C., some 67 years after his enslavement at the fall of Jerusalem in 605 B.C. This was a truly magnificent record of faithful service to God and the reigning emperors. If he was born circa 620 B.C., he would have been about 15 years old when he was carried off to Babylon, and consequently well over 80 years old when he died. His latest prophecy is chapter 10, which is dated to the third year of Cyrus, king of Persia, that is, 536 B.C. In many significant ways he was the power behind much that took place during those years, and has influenced all subsequent history to this day. How often God has chosen just one faithful man to fulfil His will in this world, so that the glory might be His alone!

7. *Its Supposed Historical Problems*

The Book of Daniel has been put in the 'critics' den', just as Daniel was put by his enemies in the lions' den. But, like Daniel himself, the book has survived the ordeal intact and has been largely confirmed by competent scholarship. A few historical facts referred to in the book have not yet been verified from non-canonical sources, but others have been verified completely. So that we can say with assurance that the Book of Daniel is what it claims to be, a vital and important primary historical document from the sixth century B.C., and in every way reliable.

An example of a supposed historical problem in the book which has subsequently been confirmed and clarified is the reference in chapter 5 to Belshazzar being the son of Nebuchadnezzar. Belshazzar was once unknown in the secular sources, but has now been discovered in the cuneiform documents. In the secular sources he is known as 'the king's son', in fact, the son of Nabonidus, a usurper and not related to Nebuchadnezzar by blood. But in Semitic idiom that notice is actually accurate, even if no blood relationship can be proved. Further, Belshazzar is correctly called 'king' in Daniel, because he was exercising royal functions in the name of his father, Nabonidus. A cuneiform source states that Nabonidus entrusted the kingship to his son, Belshazzar. This co-regency between Nabonidus and Belshazzar perfectly explains why Daniel would have become only the 'third ruler' in the kingdom, rather than the second. The accuracy of Scripture is thus confirmed, not denied.

An example of a supposed historical problem in the book which has not yet been completely solved by reference to secular sources is the reference in chapter 5 verse 31 to Darius the Mede at the age of sixty-two taking the kingdom from Belshazzar. The name 'Darius the Mede' is so far unknown in the secular sources. But he has been identified with Gubaru, the governor appointed by Cyrus over Babylon. Gubaru is frequently mentioned in cuneiform documents during the following fourteen years as 'Governor of Babylon and the Region Beyond the River'. This view accords with Daniel 5.31-6.3, where Darius the Mede received the kingdom as a sub-king from Cyrus the Great, and organized it under 120 satraps with three administrators over them. Scholarly believers await confirmation of this from secular sources, but are prepared in the meantime to accept the statements of acknowledged Scripture without question.

8. *The Keys to its Correct Interpretation*
The correct interpretation of the book depends upon four basic presuppositions.

1) *That the book is authentic and a genuine composition of Daniel in the sixth century B.C.* This has been disputed by scholarly unbelievers on the basis that apocalyptic literature did not develop until some centuries later in the Greek period. But other Biblical books from the earlier centuries, such as Zechariah, and parts of Isaiah and Ezekiel, contain apocalyptic passages, so that this argument is invalid.

2) *That predictive prophecy is not only possible, but also the warp and woof of Biblical apocalyptic literature.* To deny that God can predict and has predicted the future in the way the Book of Daniel claims to is evidence of unbelief. This fundamental unbelief lies behind the negative criticism of Daniel's prophecies. The only way for such scholars to explain the meticulously accurate prophecies of the Book of Daniel is to suppose that they date from a later century, and to deny that Daniel wrote them by positing a pseudo-Daniel in the second century B.C. This, however, is a poor expedient, since many of the prophecies concern predictions of the first and second advents of Christ, the Great Tribulation, and the future of Israel, some of which have definitely been fulfilled already in detail, and some of which remain to be fulfilled in days still future to us. Scripture asserts that true prophets do predict the future accurately, while false prophets do not and cannot. True prophets are the mouthpiece of the God who controls all history.

The humble believer in God is simply enthralled by the vast panorama of prophetic revelation contained in the Book of Daniel.

3) *That God has a future for Daniel's people Israel.* This is the key truth that opens this book and all other biblical prophecy. No later prophecies in the New Testament can be correctly understood without accepting this truth, and acquiring a knowledge of the Book of Daniel. The Lord Jesus Christ Himself referred to the book in His Olivet discourse in Matthew chapter 24, where He predicted that 'the abomination of desolation, spoken of by Daniel the prophet' will be set up in the temple in the middle of the Tribulation. The Book of Revelation derives its basic structure from the seventieth week of Daniel's prophecy of the Seventy Weeks in chapter 9. Daniel's prophecies reveal that God has not finished with His earthly people Israel by any means; that although they have a long hard pathway of divine discipline to tread for their sins, God will yet remember them for blessing in a future day, and that the Gentile nations also must one day bow the knee to Israel's God, who is their God too. In the New Testament Romans chapters 9-11 confirm this truth. God's promises to Israel never have been, nor ever will be, cancelled or transferred to the New Testament Church. The Church has not replaced Israel in God's purposes, but has a parallel, but separate, function in them as God's heavenly people, as opposed to Israel, God's earthly people. The Book of Daniel can be read and accepted as it stands, concerning both the Gentiles and Israel, and needs no reinterpreting in terms of the Church, which is nowhere revealed in it. Church saints today delight to read the Book of Daniel for instruction in God's purposes for the future of this world and for exhortations to godly living like Daniel and his friends, but they do not see themselves in the book. Rather, they see that events in the present age are all pointing towards the fulfilment of Daniel's prophecies in the not too distant future. This causes us to lift up our heads and expect our Saviour to come for us very soon. Maranatha!

4) *That the book is to be understood as literally as possible, consistently with the use of symbolical language in the apocalyptic sections.* Some of these symbols are explained in the book, while others are not explained there, but can be understood to some extent by referring to other Scriptures. They represent actual characters, objects, and events, not just vague abstract ideas. This principle is consistent with the way in which all other Scripture is meant to be interpreted. Evidently, real and powerful spiritual forces were at work in the events of world history in Daniel's day, and have been ever since. Truly, as has often been stated, 'History is His Story'! The literal understanding and acceptance of the Book of Daniel is both essential and most spiritually profitable to our souls today. Having said that, chapter 12 of the book indicates that Daniel himself failed to understand the significance of all that he saw and heard, since to him and to all his generation the book was to be 'sealed up' until the 'time of the end'. The very fact that we today can understand the book fairly clearly and see that its events will probably take place quite soon is evidence that we are living in days very near to the 'time of the end'. This gives us renewed hope in the promises of God to ourselves, as well as to Israel and the Gentile nations. The coming of the Lord is certainly drawing near. Hallelujah!

9. Its Two Languages
The Book of Daniel is written in two different languages: Hebrew, the language of the Jews; and Biblical Aramaic, the international language of the Middle East in the days of the Babylonian and Persian empires. Chapters 1-2.3 are written in Hebrew; chapters 2.4-7.28 are written in Aramaic; while chapters 8-12 revert to Hebrew. The book is thus split fairly evenly between the two languages. It should be observed that the Gentile Aramaic language is used to convey to us the histories and prophecies which most closely concern the Gentile world kingdoms during the 'Times of the Gentiles', while Hebrew, the language of the Jewish exiles, is used to convey the record of the Lord's programme for the future of His earthly people Israel during those same times. The introductory chapter, which

relates how a few faithful Jewish captives resisted pressure to compromise with their captors' Babylonian ways, is significantly also in Hebrew. There is thus spiritual instruction to be gained from observing which language is used to record which parts of the book. There is nothing purely arbitrary or accidental about this feature of Daniel's prophecy.

10. Its Analysis

The Book of Daniel can therefore conveniently be divided into major sections, partly on the basis of the languages in which it was written, and partly on the basis of the nature of its contents. Two main ways of analysing the book have been suggested, both of which have much merit. Firstly, and most simply, many commentators divide the book into: 1) chapters 1-6, labelling these the historical section; followed by: 2) chapters 7-12, which contain Daniel's visions, largely concerning his people Israel and their future. But secondly, and following the different language sections in the book, others suggest that the book should be divided into: 1) chapter 1 (in Hebrew), the introduction to Daniel and his friends; 2) chapters 2-7 (in Aramaic), which comprise the dreams of Nebuchadnezzar, the histories of the Babylonian and Persian kings, and the vision of Daniel concerning the Gentile world kingdoms; and 3) chapters 8-12 (in Hebrew again) , which contain Daniel's further visions concerning God's future programme for Israel during the remainder of the Times of the Gentiles.

11. Its Chronology

We should observe from the dates assigned to all the chapters in the book that, whilst there is an overall chronological progression in the book from Daniel's youth in chapter 1, which must be dated to 605 B.C. and immediately subsequent years, through to his extreme old age in chapter 12, the 530's B.C., not all the book follows a strictly chronological pattern of thought. The two visions of chapters 7 and 8 from early in Belshazzar's reign chronologically precede chapters 5 and 6, dated at the end of Belshazzar's reign and the beginning of Darius's reign respectively.

12. Its Subject Arrangement Summarised

We may, therefore, expect to find some subject arrangement within the book as a whole. This has been expressed perhaps most succinctly in M.F. Unger's suggested analysis at the beginning of his commentary on the book, as follows: 1) _The Times of Gentile Dominion over Israel_, chapters 1-7; 2) _Israel's Future in relation to Gentile Dominion_, chapters 8-12.

Bearing all this in mind, then, let us consider chapter 1.

CHAPTER 1

The Making of a Man of God

Chapter 1 forms a very suitable introduction to the Book of Daniel. Daniel in this chapter would probably have been a teenager, about fifteen years old. The kingdom of Judah is here seen to be conquered by the Babylonian king Nebuchadnezzar, who proceeded to carry away the most able of the Jewish young men to his own country for re-education in Babylonian ways with a view to redeployment in the administration of his expanding empire. Daniel and his three friends, Hananiah, Mishael, and Azariah, qualified for inclusion in this deportation to Babylon, since they were exceptionally gifted both in body and in mind. But, and this Nebuchadnezzar had not realised concerning them, they were also exceptionally devoted and faithful to the Lord their God, young as they were at the time of their ordeal. The chapter does in fact demonstrate the way in which God prepared them all, and Daniel in particular, for future service not only in the top administrative posts of the Babylonian Empire, but also in His own far-reaching purposes both for the future world empires and the future of His own people, Israel, now exiled from their land. In short, we see here some of the ways in which God prepares a man of God for his later service for Him.

The Date and Circumstances of the Beginning of the Book
The first verse of the book indicates that the author Daniel used the Babylonian method of reckoning time, rather than that of his former homeland, Judah. According to Babylonian reckoning of a king's reign, his accession year was not counted

in the total number of the years of his reign, whereas in Judah the accession year was counted. Thus, this verse does not conflict with the statement in Jeremiah chapter 25 verse 1 that Nebuchadnezzar captured Jerusalem in the fourth year of Jehoiakim's reign, rather than the third year of Jehoiakim's reign, as stated here. There is no contradiction, if one understands that, whereas Jeremiah is using the Jewish/Palestinian method of reckoning a king's reign, Daniel, as part of the Babylonian administration, was using the Babylonian system. In a book which begins with the first year of the Times of the Gentiles, namely, 605 B.C., and ends in chapter 12 with the conclusion of that same period at the Second Coming of Christ to reign, this is entirely appropriate. Jeremiah, on the other hand, was writing as a Jewish patriot as well as a prophet of the Lord. It should be noted, incidentally, that this year 605 B.C., mentioned in both Jeremiah chapter 25 verse 1 and Daniel chapter 1 verse 1, is pivotal in Old Testament chronology as a whole. From it other dates can be worked out before and after this event, which is fixed according to the secular historical sources also.

At the time of his first capture of Jerusalem Nebuchadnezzar was not yet actually the king of Babylon, but the heir apparent of his father, Nabopolassar, and his father's army commander. But shortly after this event his father died, leaving the empire to the care of Nebuchadnezzar. So the word 'king' here is used in anticipation of his imminent accession to his father's throne. It is in no way a historical inaccuracy on the part of the author of the Book of Daniel, as some scholarly unbelievers have claimed, but an example of the literary figure of speech called 'prolepsis'. Nebuchadnezzar was soon to be king at the time of the fall of Jerusalem.

By the Lord's sovereign permission, Nebuchadnezzar took some of the vessels of the temple of the Lord to Babylon, and put them in the temples of his heathen idols. Although he thus attributed his success in battle to his own gods, he was going to learn later in chapter 4 that his position and success were due entirely to the Lord's sovereign will, not to his own prowess, nor that of his idols. From his understanding of the preaching of the Hebrew prophets he would have known that he was the Lord's instrument in disciplining the people of God for their sins against Him, but he took some years to accept fully the reality and implications of this fact.

The chapter may be conveniently divided into four sections: 1) *Daniel's Removal from his homeland to Babylon*, verses 1-7; 2) *Daniel's Resolve not to compromise with Babylonian ways*, verses 8-16; 3) *Daniel and his friends' Remarkable Success in their Education in Babylon*, verses 17-20; and 4) *Daniel's Reward for his Faithfulness*, verse 21. In the first three sections there is a marked emphasis on the sovereignty of God in his life, indicated by the repetition of the phrase 'the Lord, or God, gave', in verses 2, 9, and 17.

1. *Daniel's Removal from his homeland to Babylon, vv.1-7*
First of all, the direction of Daniel's life was determined by the fact stated in verse 2, that 'The Lord gave Jehoiakim King of Judah into his (Nebuchadnezzar's) hand'. Judah, as well as the northern kingdom of Israel earlier, had so sinned against the Lord their God that He allowed the Gentile nations to invade and conquer them. Israel as a whole had disobeyed the commandments of the Mosaic Covenant and Law, and had also neglected to observe the requirement to let their land lie fallow every seven years, the sabbatical years. For this, according to the predictions of Deuteronomy chapter 28, they were to be removed from their land and exiled as slaves in their enemies' lands; first Assyria for the northern kingdom, then Babylon for the southern kingdom here. This explains why Daniel's circumstances were so completely changed during his youth, as were those of his three close friends and many other young men of his age. All their links with their former homes were suddenly broken, and they were subjected to pressure to conform to the life-style of the Babylonians. Their names, which all had meanings in Hebrew relating to the Lord their God, were

changed to reflect the worship of the Babylonian gods. Daniel, 'God is my Judge', was changed to Belteshazzar, 'Bel's prince'; Hananiah, 'mercy of the Lord', was changed to Shadrach, possibly meaning 'command of Aku'; Mishael, 'who is what God is', was changed to Meshach, 'who is like Aku?'; and Azariah, 'whom the Lord helps', was changed to Abednego, 'servant of Nebo'. This they could not prevent, and simply accepted as from the Lord's overruling hand. But when the Babylonian authorities began to exert pressure on them to compromise their faith and eat food offered to idols, or at least unclean according to the Levitical dietary laws, they had a big decision to make; whether to yield to the pressure to compromise, or to make a stand for their God on conscientious grounds and refuse to be defiled by the rich royal, but unclean, food presented to them.

2. Daniel's Resolve not to Compromise with Babylonian Ways, vv.8-16

Daniel decided to stand firm on his principles and refused to eat the king's food, and was followed in this by his three friends. At this point God sovereignly stepped into the situation again, according to verse 9, and gave Daniel favour and compassion in the sight of the chief of the eunuchs, or court officers. Without this factor the situation might well have resulted in the summary deaths of the four young men. But the chief of the eunuchs was prepared to listen to Daniel's polite request for a change of diet on a ten-day trial basis in spite of the fact that he himself might be in danger of displeasing the king and losing his own life. Note that Daniel's request was couched in tactful and courteous terms, not in any arrogant or self-assertive manner. God had overruled, but Daniel had his part to play in the handling of a delicate situation. The consequence of the ten-day trial period, during which the four friends ate only vegetables, permissible according to the Levitical Law, was that the four friends were vindicated in their stand for godliness, and looked much better in health than their fellows who had continued to eat the king's contaminated food. 'Them that honour me, I will honour', the

Lord had said in 1 Samuel 2.30, and Daniel here proved this promise of Scripture. As a result, the four friends continued to eat their permitted diet until the end of their period of preparation for the king's presence.

3. Daniel and his friends' Remarkable Success in their Education in Babylon, vv.17-20

Thirdly, then, in verse 17 God sovereignly gave all four young men learning and skill in all literature and wisdom, but in addition granted Daniel an extra gift, 'understanding in all visions and dreams', which were considered important in those times by most of the peoples of the ancient world. These gifts, so sovereignly given to the young trainees, gave them a decisive advantage over their fellow-students when the time came for them to go in to the king and be examined by him. The four came out top of the examinations, and were given responsible jobs closest to the king.

The way of obedience is always the key to blessing, although it can lead us into difficult situations. Had Daniel not resolved to avoid compromising his godly convictions from the Word of God, God would not have intervened to relieve the situation, and the four friends would have been absorbed into the godless life-style of the Babylonian court. As it turned out, both Daniel and his friends were able to exert a decisive influence for the Lord their God at the heart of their natural enemies' administration. Daniel himself was soon able to use his God-given gift of interpreting dreams to reveal to the most powerful ruler of his day, and through him to us today, His own purposes for the future direction of world history, and the future of his own captive people Israel.

The four friends accepted certain unavoidable aspects of their situation, such as their change of official names, and their very presence in an enemy's land, as the consequence of their people's disobedience to God. But when their personal convictions concerning their conduct were challenged, they sought graciously to avoid compromising their faith and the Word of God. This is an example for younger, and older, believers today to follow, especially when they are removed by unavoidable circumstances from their homes and loved ones to ungodly environments. Those who do make a stand on the basis of clear Scripture often find that the Lord overrules their situation, and sovereignly helps them in it. His own glory is at stake in the vindication of His own faithful people. Very often the most tested younger Christians turn out to be the most used in the Lord's service, and also are able to prosper in the secular sphere as well. Not all of us can be, nor are expected to become, 'high-flyers' like these four young men were, but all of us can prove the truths taught here in a somewhat humbler sphere of life.

4. *Daniel's Reward for his Faithfulness, v.21*
The final verse of the chapter concerning Daniel continuing to the first year of King Cyrus, that is right through the period of the Babylonian Empire and into the first years of the succeeding Persian Empire, is testimony in itself both to his faithfulness and to God's honouring him as His devoted servant. Because Daniel had had a 'purpose firm' in his youth, and had resisted the temptation to compromise with the unclean ways of his captors, God preserved him all through the long years of the Babylonian Captivity, the corruption and violence of the Babylonian administration, and even allowed him to be instrumental in bringing about the beginning of the restoration of a remnant of faithful Jews to their Promised Land in 538 B.C. The verse does not mean that Daniel died in the first year of Cyrus' reign, but that he succeeded in surviving the dangers of high position right through to that year. He did in fact live at least until the third year of Cyrus, 536 B.C., according to the vision of chapter 10 verse 1, and even then his book may have remained to be written during a further last few years. He was probably nearer ninety than eighty when he did eventually die.

What an encouragement he is to all younger believers today

especially! Daniel and his companions represent the godly remnant of their day who preserved the true testimony of God untarnished even in dark days of apostasy and divine judgement. Their noble example will encourage the future godly remnant of Israel to endure to the end during the trials of the coming 'time of the end'. So now let us today, 'Dare to be a Daniel, Dare to stand alone, Dare to have a purpose firm, And dare to make it known!'

God's Panoramic Revelation of Future World History

The prophecies of the Book of Daniel show a definite development from chapter to chapter. After each revelation, Daniel seems to have meditated deeply and inquired further into certain aspects of what he had learned. This in turn brought further revelations. Each successive prophecy built upon that which had gone before, but added further detail. The revelation of chapter 2, while being the simplest of the prophecies in the book, is the foundation of them all. It must be mastered if the rest of the book is to be understood. In fact, this chapter contains one of the most basic of all the prophecies in the entire Bible. It gives an outline of the history of the Gentile nations from Daniel's time, from 605 B.C., right down to the First Coming of Christ, then jumps on to His Second Coming.

The large Aramaic section of the book begins with chapter 2 verse 4 and continues through to the end of chapter 7 verse 28. It was appropriate that the major part of the book which dealt with the history of the Times of the Gentiles should be written in the contemporary Gentile international language. The Authorised Version calls Aramaic 'Syriack' here in verse 4. Another word for Aramaic is 'Chaldee', which is used in some dictionaries and concordances.

Chapter 2 divides fairly clearly into five main sections, as follows:-

1) *Nebuchadnezzar's Frustration concerning his Image Dream,* vv.1-12;
2) *God's Revelation of the Dream to Daniel,* vv.13-30;
3) *Its Description by Daniel,* vv.31-35;
4) *Its Interpretation by Daniel,* vv.36-45;
5) *Nebuchadnezzar's Response,* vv.46-49.

The Problem of the Chapter's date

According to verse 1 this incident occurred 'in the second year of the reign of Nebuchadnezzar', and after the completion of the four friends' three-year period of training mentioned in chapter 1. How can this have happened only in the second year of Nebuchadnezzar's reign and not later than that? Scholarly believers have sought a solution to this apparent problem as follows. 1) Babylonian methods of reckoning Nebuchadnezzar's reign were being used, as in chapter 1, so that his accession year, September 605-March/April 604 B.C., was not counted in the total. 2) March/April 602 B.C. would thus be reckoned as the end of his second year. 3) Daniel's training period would have extended from the Summer of 605 B.C. until sometime in 602 B.C., and the three years may not have been three full years, but similar to our somewhat shorter academic years. 4) Daniel may have been called upon as soon as he had completed his training, perhaps in Spring 602 B.C. The problem is thus not insoluble, and so the recorded date can be relied upon entirely.

1. Nebuchadnezzar's Frustration concerning his Image Dream, vv.1-12

'Nebuchadnezzar dreamed dreams', and was greatly troubled to know their meaning. It is significant that this vision of the future was granted not to Daniel, but to the first representative of Gentile world power, who had recently conquered the Israelite theocracy. Nebuchadnezzar was now God's vice-regent in the world, according to verse 37 and Jeremiah chapter 25 verse 9, having taken over that role from the kings of Israel. But Nebuchadnezzar needed Daniel, the faithful Jew, to reveal the meaning of the dream to him. God was telling him that, although he was very privileged to have the position he held, in the end all Gentile rule in the earth would be destroyed by the coming of Christ.

It is not completely certain whether Nebuchadnezzar had forgotten the dream he had, or whether he did remember it, and simply wanted to test his wise men's ability to reveal it to him. The issue turns on the meaning of a short phrase in the Aramaic which is repeated in verses 5 and 8. The Authorised Version translates it, 'The thing is gone from me', which would imply that he had definitely forgotten the contents of his dream. But many more recent versions translate it to mean, 'The word from me is firm', which implies that he had not forgotten the dream at all, but still wished to be told both its contents and meaning by his wise men. Most recent commentators favour the latter view, but the matter is not completely proven. Perhaps Nebuchadnezzar had come to distrust his close advisers and took this opportunity to test both their honesty and ability. Humanly speaking, he had set them an impossible task, and they protested about it, but the king decided to enforce his threat of execution when they failed to answer him satisfactorily.

2. God's Revelation of the Dream to Daniel, vv.13-30
So Daniel and his three friends became involved, since they were subject to the same penalty as the heathen wise men. Whereas the wise men were powerful astrologers who used occult practices to determine the future, the four godly Jews had access to the true God of heaven, who had in fact given the king the dream in the first place. Daniel, again, is the leader in the story, taking the initiative with Arioch, the king's executioner. Tactfully, if urgently, he requested some further time to consult both his friends and his God in prayer. The record of the four friends praying together is the first occurrence of a formal prayer-meeting in Scripture. Here we see the effectiveness of the fervent prayers of righteous men united in their requests to God. In fact, Nebuchadnezzar's arbitrary decision to test his wise men is a clear example of God's

overruling sovereignty in the book. For that method of handling the situation not only exposed the fraudulence of the occult astrologers, but also enabled God to demonstrate Daniel's genuineness, and so redounded to His own greater glory.

God's answer to the four friends' united prayer was immediate. God revealed the mystery of the dream to Daniel in a vision the following night. Note that God is here called 'the God of heaven', because Israel was outside of the Promised Land and God's glory was no longer resident in the temple at Jerusalem as it had been before the Exile. Throughout the Times of the Gentiles He rules the world from heaven, not through Israel on earth.

Daniel's reaction to the answer to their prayers was very exemplary: first, worship; then, thanksgiving; and only after that swift action to remedy their plight with the king. Daniel, then, praised God for His wisdom and power to control the future, to reveal the unknown, and in particular to reveal to him 'the king's matter', that is, both the contents of the dream and its meaning, so that their lives might be saved. Incidentally, God was also being merciful to the heathen wise men, since Daniel's intervention had saved their lives too.

Without further delay Daniel approached Arioch with his good news, and Arioch brought Daniel into the king's presence hastily to save the situation. Nebuchadnezzar asked Daniel if he was able to reveal the dream to him, and to give a correct interpretation of it. This gave Daniel a good opportunity to give glory to the one true God in heaven by stating that his wisdom in this matter came entirely from God, and that Nebuchadnezzar should not expect his wise men to be able to explain it. He went on to state that this one true God was making known to Nebuchadnezzar what would happen in the latter days. Here the fact emerges that, as Daniel stated, Nebuchadnezzar had been worried about the future of his kingdom. God was now revealing this future to him. Daniel then disclaimed any merit of his own in the revelations he was about to explain to the king. Rather, God was being gracious to Nebuchadnezzar in his perplexity.

3. Its Description by Daniel, vv.31-35
Nebuchadnezzar had seen in his dream a great image or statue, a kind of colossus in the form of a man. Its splendour was excellent and its appearance frightening. The head of the image was made of fine gold. Other lower parts of the image were made of stronger, but less valuable materials. The chest and arms were made of silver, the belly and thighs of brass, or rather bronze. The legs were made of iron, while its feet were made of iron mixed with clay. The king saw a great stone crash into the feet of the image and completely destroy it all. This stone then grew into a great mountain which filled the whole earth.

4. Its Interpretation by Daniel, vv.36-45
Nebuchadnezzar's image portrayed Gentile world power over Israel as a series of four successive kingdoms or empires. The Times of the Gentiles began with the capture of Jerusalem by Nebuchadnezzar in 605 B.C. and will end with the Second Coming of Christ. The Lord Jesus Himself referred to 'the Times of the Gentiles' as the period during which the Jewish people would be 'led away captive into all nations, and Jerusalem will be trampled by the Gentiles', that is, controlled by them; Luke 21.24.

<u>The First (Babylonian) Empire</u>
In the prophecies of Daniel, a king and his kingdom are sometimes spoken of interchangeably (compare Daniel chapter 7 verse 17 with chapter 7 verse 23). Daniel interpreted the head of gold as representing Nebuchadnezzar, and hence also his Babylonian Empire. The gold symbolised monarchy. Nebuchadnezzar was an absolute monarch, answering to no parliament, courts, or electorate. He ruled supreme. In this sense his form of government appeared to be the most precious, like gold, although it was actually quite despotic. Nebuchadnezzar's

dominion over mankind and the bird and animal creation, referred to in verse 38, was really the same dominion as was given to un-fallen Adam in Genesis chapter 1 verse 28 and chapter 2 verses 19-20, and lost through the Fall. This dominion was temporarily delegated to Nebuchadnezzar and the Gentile world powers, but because they have abused their privilege, it will be taken from them by Christ as the Son of Man, who will, at His Second Coming, restore the lost inheritance to mankind.

The Second (Medo-Persian) Empire

Daniel said that the chest and arms of silver represented a kingdom that would arise after Babylon and be inferior to it. Daniel lived to see the Babylonian Empire replaced by the Medo-Persian Empire as a result of the conquest of Babylon in 539 B.C. The Medes united with the Persians under Cyrus the Great to establish it; see Daniel chapter 5 verse 28 and chapter 8 verse 20. It was larger in area and more powerful than the Babylonian Empire, just as silver is more plentiful and stronger than gold. But, at the same time, it was inferior to it in its form of government, just as silver is less valuable than gold. For, unlike Nebuchadnezzar, the Persian emperors were not absolute monarchs, but answerable to the law; see Daniel chapter 6 verses 14-17. In fact, the phrase 'the law of the Medes and Persians', referring to its unchanging nature, is proverbial today. The Persian Empire dominated the known world for 200 years, from 539 to 336 B.C.

The Third (Greek) Empire

The third metal of the belly and thighs represented the Greek Empire founded by Alexander the Great in 336 B.C. Although only twenty-years old when he succeeded to the throne of Macedonia, Alexander swiftly conquered the whole of the Persian Empire in the next thirteen years from Egypt to India. When he died at the early age of nearly thirty-three, his four Greek generals divided his empire between themselves. They and their successors ruled as Grecian kingdoms for the next

250 years, until it gradually fell to the rising Roman Empire. Although Daniel does not here name this third empire, in chapters 8 and 11 he does name it and predicts its course in amazing detail. Although the Greek Empire was wider again than the preceding empires in extent, it was inferior in its quality of government to both the Babylonian and the Medo-Persian Empires, just as bronze is inferior to gold and silver, although it is both more plentiful and stronger than either of them. For in Greece individual influence acquired by personal achievement counted for much in its rise and maintenance; there was no absolute monarchy or rigid adherence to law.

The Fourth (Roman) Empire

The fourth empire of iron, then iron and clay, clearly represents the overwhelming military might of the Roman Empire, which gradually spread east and west until in the first century A.D., when Christ came the first time, it covered the whole of the then-known world. It was the most extensive and strongest of the four empires, like iron, but, also like iron, the most inferior and commonest of the four in terms of quality of government. For under it the ordinary citizens acquired many rights which would have been unthinkable under the previous three empires. The clay mixed with the iron in the feet and toes suggests an even further advance of democratic principles in the final stages of Roman rule, speaking of an awkward mixture of democratic rights and dictatorial power.

Now we in the Western World value the liberalising tendencies of democratic government, and derive some spiritual freedoms from it which enable us to propagate the gospel and live as Christians securely in many countries. But we should recognise that democracy is not really God's ideal method of government in the world; rather His own benevolent, but absolute, monarchy. And Christians in Scripture are expected to live under all sorts of governments, whether oppressive or benevolent, quietly submitting to their authority, unless their laws contravene God's laws in His Word.

When we come to the parallel vision in chapter 7, we shall see that this fourth empire, the Roman Empire, has two distinct phases. The earlier phase is portrayed by the legs of iron, while the latter phase is seen in the feet and toes of iron and clay. Now between the two phases lies a long interval, which includes our present day, when the Roman Empire is not in existence. This interval has often been called 'the great parenthesis', or 'prophetic gap', because this and other prophecies pass over it without mentioning it. In this gap lies the present New Testament Church age, the Age of Grace beginning with Pentecost and ending with the Rapture of the Church. The important point to grasp is that the Church Age is nowhere referred to directly, or in prophecy, in the Old Testament. Paul says in his epistles (notably Ephesians chapter 3 verses 1-10 and Colossians chapter 1 verse 26) that the Church was a mystery hidden in God from ages and generations, and only now revealed through the New Testament prophets like himself. The most the Old Testament contains of the Church are some typological allusions to it, but nothing clear and direct.

The ten toes of the image are mentioned in Daniel chapter 2 verse 42. It may safely be assumed that they have the same significance as the ten horns described in the parallel vision in chapter 7 verses 7 and 24, and referred to again in Revelation chapter 13 verse 1 and Revelation chapter 17 verses 3 and 12-17. These horns represent ten kings who will arise within the fourth (Roman) empire in its later phase, which is still future to us. More is said about them than all the preceding kingdoms put together, thus indicating their relative importance. The reason is that they represent the final and most inferior form of government, which will produce the personal Antichrist/Man of Sin/Beast from the sea, the acme of lawlessness, who will defy God and set himself up as God to be worshipped in His place. That is the goal of the Satanic world system represented by the colossus image.

The identity of the ten kings and their kingdoms has long been conjectured, but escapes us all at present. The current gradual formation of the European Union since the surely significant Treaty of Rome in 1957 is probably relevant to the discussion, since it represents a kind of reformation of the old Roman Empire. But it is unclear at present just how extensive that Union will eventually become; whether it will include countries in the Middle East as well as most European countries; whether it will extend westwards to include the Americas, or not; and whether it will one day be given realigned boundaries within its total area to include just ten kingdoms in all. Although it is probably the precursor to the kingdoms taken over by the Antichrist, we cannot predict just how it will develop in the nearer future. However, there is unlikely to be another later similar development of worldwide empire than the current movement. That is an indication of how near the end times we are today.

Now according to other Scriptures there will be at least some other players on the chess-board of these end time events. These are: the king of the north, traditionally Iraq/Syria/identified with the latter-day 'Assyrian' of the prophetical books; the king of the south, traditionally Egypt and its allies in the Middle East and Africa; the kings of the east, probably from eastern Asia/China/India and related countries; and Gog and Magog from the far north in relation to Israel, and thought by many to be Russia and her northern allies. This means that the ten-kingdom confederacy of the Antichrist will not be the only empire in the world at the end times, and that all these other kingdoms will exist separately from the Antichrist's world empire. However, it is still true to say that for most of the end times, which consist of the seven years of Tribulation, the ten-kingdom empire will be the most powerful one on the overall world scene. Although it will be challenged by the other players, it will remain dominant until the Second Coming of Christ. These factors may help us in considering the likely eventual development of the Antichrist's ten-toed world empire out of the current world scene.

The fourth part of the image, therefore, represents the fourth (Roman) empire, first as it existed at the time of Christ's first coming in the sixty-ninth week of Daniel's vision in chapter 9 verses 26-27, and secondly as it will exist in the future in its revived form during the seventieth week of Tribulation. The present Church age is simply passed over without any mention in the sequence of the prophecy.

The Destruction of the Image and the Advent of the Fifth and Final Kingdom

Nebuchadnezzar's awesome image was struck on the feet by 'a stone...cut out without hands', and completely destroyed. It was in fact top-heavy by reason of its constituent metals, and so easily toppled. Christ will fulfil this part of the dream at His Second Coming, when He will demolish Gentile power; Psalm 2 verses 7-9 and Revelation chapter 19 verse 15. The phrase 'cut out without hands' means that the stone that Nebuchadnezzar saw was not cut out from a quarry by human hands. It suggests the supernatural birth of Jesus Christ, born of a virgin under the overshadowing of the Holy Spirit; Luke chapter 1 verses 30-31 and 34-35. Christ's origin was divine and un-originated. The angel Gabriel told the virgin Mary that her child would eventually take the throne of King David and rule over Israel for ever; Luke chapter 1 verses 32-33. Daniel chapter 2 verse 44 tells us that Christ's rule will extend over all nations. This is the meaning of verse 35, 'the stone that struck the image became a great mountain and filled the whole earth'. In that coming day, Jesus Christ, who was once 'the stone that the builders rejected', will become 'King of kings and Lord of lords'; Revelation chapter 19 verse 16. From Genesis chapter 49 onwards through Scripture Christ is consistently represented by the figure of 'the Stone'. He is the solid foundation of all God's purposes.

So God was making known to Nebuchadnezzar the long-term future and end of his kingdom, which he had been concerned to understand. And God through Daniel affirmed in chapter 2 verse 45 that the dream was certain in its meaning and trustworthy as to its interpretation. Subsequent world history has confirmed this abundantly.

Chapter 7 presents the interpretation of a parallel vision of the same sequence of world empires from a different point of view, God's point of view, as opposed to man's point of view here in chapter 2. In chapter 7 the same world empires as are here represented by an impressive colossus containing valuable metals are described as unclean wild animals which devour all before them with great ferocity and cruelty. That is how God views all world empires and emperors.

5. Nebuchadnezzar's response, vv.46-49

At this amazing revelation to him by God through Daniel Nebuchadnezzar fell prostrate and worshipped Daniel, because Daniel to him represented the one true God. Daniel did not wrongly compromise here, but accepted Nebuchadnezzar's homage as God's representative in revealing the matter of the dream. Nebuchadnezzar acknowledged God as 'a God of gods' and 'a Lord of kings' as a result of this incident. He was later in chapter 4 to come to a still fuller and personal faith in God. Immediately, Nebuchadnezzar promoted Daniel to high office in the administration of his empire. Daniel in turn took the opportunity to request that his three friends be promoted to similar high office in the administration of the province of Babylon. Daniel himself 'sat in the gate of the king', a very senior post in the empire. So their prayer of faith was rewarded and their sufferings, at least for a time, alleviated. Their godliness had been rewarded with the favour of the greatest despot of all time. And, under God's providential hand, it gave all of them abundant opportunity to exert a godly influence upon the affairs of state and to witness to the truth of their 'God in heaven'.

God still delights to tell those who trust, love, and obey Him His secrets concerning the future. Through predictive prophecy He is both encouraging His own believing people and warning unbelievers of the fate that awaits them if they do not repent and turn from their wicked ways. The study of prophetic Scripture is not only enthralling and revealing; it is honouring to God and profitable to ourselves as we are guided by its revelations. To neglect prophecy is to refuse to listen when God wants to tell us many things.

Note on the Chiastic Structure of the Aramaic section of Daniel, chapters 2-7

Some commentators have pointed out that there is a definite and instructive 'chiastic' structure discernable within the Aramaic section of Daniel's prophecy. A 'chiasmus' is a figure of speech involving two pairs of words in which the order of the words used in the first pair is reversed in the second pair. If this word order is drawn as a diagram AB,BA and the similar parts are linked by lines, then the resulting pattern looks like the Greek letter 'Chi', X, which is like a diagonal cross. Therefore, it is called a 'chiasmus'. It is a 'crosswise arrangement' of words in a sentence, a reverse parallelism. There are examples of this arrangement in various Bible sentences, such as Philemon verse 5 and 2 Thessalonians chapter 1 verses 6 and 7. Here in Daniel chapters 2-7 the same chiastic arrangement is found in the thought structure of these six chapters. For chapter 2 with its image dream corresponds to the parallel vision of the four wild beasts in chapter 7, both describing and predicting the same future world empires. Chapter 3, with its description of the trial of the three young friends in the fiery furnace for refusing to worship Nebuchadnezzar's golden image of himself, and their vindication, finds its counterpart in chapter 6, where Daniel is delivered from the lions' den after refusing to pray only to the Persian king. Finally, chapter 4, which relates the downfall of the proud monarch Nebuchadnezzar and his conversion to God, has its counterpart in chapter 5, where Belshazzar meets his end for sacrilege and pride at the hands of the Medo-Persian invaders, but has, in his case, no opportunity to repent. The thought structure of the whole section, ABC,CBA, is most marked. It should probably be viewed as a stamp of divine inspiration.

Note on some other Interpretations of the Dream Image

In accordance with the principles outlined in the Introduction, the interpretation of Nebuchadnezzar's dream image followed here is the Premillennial one. This fully accepts predictive prophecy concerning all events future to Daniel's day, and is the most consistently believing of the various interpretations given to this chapter. It may, however, be helpful to mention two other ways of interpreting the image dream which have been, and still are, held by many Bible students, and to point out their weaknesses. The object of doing this is to strengthen the faith of all true believers in the correctness of the usual Premillennial approach to both this Scripture, and to others related to it.

1) *The Liberal Interpretation*

Liberal theologians usually do not believe in the possibility of predictive prophecy. Therefore, they tend to interpret predicted events as if they had been written about after the events predicted have occurred in history rather than before they occur. In connection with the image dream here, this tendency leads them to interpret the second, third, and fourth empires differently from scholarly Premillennial believers. Liberal scholars try to differentiate between the Median and the Persian Empires and to say that the second empire of silver is just Media by itself, while the third empire is Persia by itself. This enables them to hold that the fourth empire is not Rome, but Greece, so that the Roman Empire does not appear anywhere in their interpretation. To admit that the fourth empire is Rome would definitely involve them in accepting predictive prophecy, since the Roman Empire was many centuries in the future from Daniel's purported day, the sixth century B.C. Rather, they hold that Daniel was a fictitious character, and that a later prophet assumed his name and wrote the book under the name of Daniel not in the sixth, but in the second century B.C., that is, after many of the events referred to in the book had already occurred. But scholarly believers have pointed out that the language and historical background assumed in the book are both consistent with an earlier, sixth century, date rather than a second century Maccabean date. Furthermore, both history and the Book of Daniel confirm that the Medo-Persian Empire was really one empire, not two. Also, many of the events predicted in the book relate to times far later than even the second century B.C., in fact, right up to the first and second comings of Christ. So the liberal scholars cannot avoid admitting the presence of predictive prophecy even on their own quite false assumptions. Their whole position is thus untenable, and can be refuted in detail by comparing the actual later histories of the world empires with the image dream here.

2) *The Amillennial and Postmillennial Interpretations*
Other scholars, many of whom are sincere believers and have written widely-read commentaries on the book, attempt to see the New Testament Church in this image dream, as they do in many other parts of Old Testament prophecy. This is a serious mistake, which leads to strange interpretations. Here, for instance, Amillennial expositors, who deny that there will be a literal millennial kingdom, simply cannot give an interpretation of the image which accords with the facts of history. In the view of both Amillennialists and some Postmillennialists, the Kingdom of God spoken of in the image dream is that which Christ inaugurated at His first coming, rather than His second coming. For they see the millennial kingdom as the present age, rather than the future golden age after Christ's second coming. This view thus inevitably cannot find any adequate explanation of the feet stage of the image, or of the corresponding period predicted in the vision of the fourth wild beast of chapter 7 verses 7-8. The confusion is compounded when a historical setting is sought for this part of the visions in the Church age, so that anyone's guess is as good as another's as to the meaning intended. The view that the millennial kingdom was introduced by Christ at His first coming also presupposes the gradual destruction of the image by the Church in the succeeding centuries, rather than its sudden, violent, and complete destruction at the Second Coming of Christ. Such a violent

destruction is totally at variance with the nature and commission of the Church. Again, we must stress that the Church is nowhere mentioned or implied in Daniel's prophecies. Israel never became the Church, nor has the Church had Israel's promises transferred to it. Israel has a literal future, according to Romans chapters 9-11, despite their disobedience and rejection of Christ. Finally, the Church has not conquered the world either religiously or politically, and has not been promised that it will do so. Instead, the present Church age is to end in the Apostasy and rebellion rather than the victory of the Church. Christ will have to intervene in judgement at His Second Coming to rectify the situation on earth. No, the literal, Premillennial interpretation of the image dream is the only one that accords with both a believing approach to the Book of Daniel and the rest of Scripture.

CHAPTER 3

Faith's Fiery Trial

In this chapter we find that the faith of Daniel's three friends is tested to the utmost limit, but proved to be genuine and vindicated by God. The circumstances of their trial of faith arose directly out of the image dream of the previous chapter.

1. Nebuchadnezzar's Golden Image
Despite his apparent acknowledgement of God at the time, Nebuchadnezzar's longer-term reaction to his image dream was both unfortunate and alarming. Not content to be told that he was the image's head of gold, his thoughts turned to self-glorification. He decided to build an image made entirely of gold which all his subjects must worship. It was really an act of self-deification. He ignored all the other features of his dream's image, including its catastrophic end, and attempted to retain his God-given power and glory indefinitely. But he was soon to learn that whoever presumes to demand for himself the glory due to God alone is sure to face His disciplinary dealings, as the present chapter proves to us.

2. Its Dedication, vv.1-7
The golden image was set up 'in the plain of Dura, in the province of Babylon'. It measured sixty cubits (at least 90 feet) in height and six cubits (at least 9 feet) in width. Nebuchadnezzar arranged a grand dedication ceremony for it, to which all the high officials of his empire were summoned. Beautiful music was provided to encourage everyone present to bow in worship before the image, and thus honour the king.

How often have good music and grand architecture accompanied false religion down the centuries to the present day! The herald who introduced the proceedings made it clear that whoever refused to worship the image would be thrown immediately into a burning fiery furnace. So the scene was set for a severe trial of faith for the faithful Jewish captives, who were obliged to be present at the ceremony.

3. *The Three Friends' Refusal to Worship it, vv.8-18*

It is unclear why Daniel was not among the congregation convened to worship the king's golden image, since it is unthinkable that, had he been present, he would not have stood firmly with his three close friends, Shadrach, Meshach, and Abednego, and with them refused to bow to it. Some time may have elapsed since the events of chapter 2, so Daniel may have been away from Babylon on the king's business elsewhere, or perhaps he was ill at the time, and so unable to be present. However, Daniel was not involved in this incident, while his three friends were fully exposed to both its temptations and its dangers.

At the very least, the three young Jews were being required to compromise their faith in God by worshipping Nebuchadnezzar's image, if not quite directly denying it. For the king's command contravened the first two commandments of the Mosaic Law, namely, those forbidding the worship of any god other than the Lord, and the making and worship of any graven image. So the young believers had a choice to make. Either they could swallow their consciences towards God and compromise, or they could refuse to compromise their faith and devotion to God and accept the dire consequences. Commendably, they chose the latter course.

The Chaldeans, that is, the Babylonian astrologers, the king's wise men, took full advantage of the situation, because they were envious of the highly-favoured Jewish captives, and reported the latter's non-compliance with the king's command.

This set in motion a rapid sequence of dramatic events. Predictably, Nebuchadnezzar was absolutely furious with the three young Jews. Who were they to defy him? Power and glory had clearly gone to his head. However, probably because they had won his respect by previous good conduct and faithful service, he gave them a second chance to comply with his command. But they remained quite resolute in their refusal to worship the golden image. In so doing they demonstrated three things. First, they demonstrated great faith and confidence in the ability of God to save them; for they said in verse 17, 'Our God whom we serve is able to deliver us'. Secondly, they recognised that God might not choose to deliver them, when they added the words of verse 18a, 'But if not...' to their previous assertion. For believers must recognise that it is not always God's will to save his people from death by persecution, or from illness. Hebrews chapter 11 verses 35-37 and 2 Corinthians chapter 12 verses 7-9 indicate this quite clearly. Like the Lord Jesus Himself in the Garden of Gethsemane, we should always add, 'Father, if it is Thy will' to our prayers; Luke chapter 22 verse 42. But, thirdly, their brave stand gave evidence of a settled determination to be true to God at all costs, whether He did choose to save their lives from the fiery furnace or not. They continued in verse 18b, 'Let it be known to you, O king, that we do not serve your gods, nor will we worship the golden image'.

4. *Their Deliverance from the Fiery Furnace, vv.19-30*
On hearing the three friends' bold, but defiant statement, Nebuchadnezzar decided to implement his threat of execution. Enraged by their disobedience, he ordered the furnace to be heated seven times hotter than its normal temperature. Of course, this would actually in normal circumstances have reduced, rather than increased, the victims' suffering, because death would have been instantaneous rather than slow and painful. In the event, the soldiers who bound the three young men and threw them into the furnace were themselves killed by the heat of the flames. But, remarkably, the fire had no effect on the servants of God. It simply burned off their ropes, but

did not even singe their hair or leave a smell of fire on their clothing. Something quite miraculous was taking place. Then, after some time, when the king looked inside the furnace, he was quite startled to see not three burnt bodies, but four men walking about inside it unharmed. He exclaimed that the fourth man was 'like the Son of God', or, in his heathen manner of understanding the phenomenon, 'like a son of the gods', a celestial being, or an angel. Probably the fourth man was a Christophany, an appearance of the pre-Incarnate Son of God in human form. God had chosen to deliver his faithful servants from certain death by miraculous means. Proud Nebuchadnezzar accepted his defeat by the one true God, whom as a Gentile he called 'the most high God', quite well, and seemed at the time to acknowledge Him, although the next chapter proves that he had still not yet fully done so. So proud is the human heart that God must use many lessons to humble us and teach us to acknowledge Him fully. The result of this trial of the three Jews' faith was that they were promoted in the administrative ranks of the province of Babylon, and nobody was permitted to say anything against the Lord their God. Thus their stand for the truth was completely vindicated.

Simple believers accept this account of the miraculous intervention of God in the situation as absolutely true and factual, not a fairy tale told for the benefit of Jews in the second century to encourage them in their struggles at that later time. For, if it did not actually happen, there is no real encouragement in the telling of the story at all. No, the divine inspiration of Scripture is at stake in the matter. God does not always deliver His people from persecution, but He both can do so, and has done so on a number of occasions to uphold the honour of His Name. Our God is an Almighty Saviour God!

A Personal Challenge
The personal challenge of the chapter comes to us with real force. In our day, as in the days of many believers down the centuries, the world exerts strong pressure on us to compromise

our faith in God in many ways. While the world cries, 'Conform, fit in, be politically correct', God says to us, 'Be not conformed to this world, but be transformed by the renewing of your mind'; see Romans chapter 12 verses 1-2. And that Scripture appeals to us to yield ourselves to God as living sacrifices to do His perfect will, the supreme motive being His great mercies shown to us in the sacrifice of Christ, His own Beloved Son. This principle applies to every aspect of our lives and behaviour, to our clothing styles, hobbies, habits, business practices, religion, and moral standards. When the pressure is on, are we willing to stand up and be counted as servants of God? If we do stand for the truth of God, we will find that God will stand with us in the resulting trials of faith. This is both the price of non-conformity, and its 'exceeding great reward'; see 2 Timothy chapter 4 verse 17 and Genesis chapter 14 verse 22 to 15 verse 1.

The Prophetic Significance of the Chapter

Now the record of the victorious trial of the young Jews' faith in this chapter is also a foreshadowing of a still greater triumph of faith in the yet future Tribulation period. For then, as never before or afterwards, the faith of the believing Jewish remnant will be tested by the fires of persecution from the Antichrist/ the Beast/the Man of Sin during his short three and a half year reign of terror, according to Revelation chapter 13. And while many believers, both Jewish and Gentile, will be martyred by him, a complete group of 144,000 specially-sealed Jewish witnesses will be preserved unharmed through all those troubled times, and be seen standing at its close on Mount Zion in the earthly Jerusalem still living and victorious over all the opposition of their enemies, according to Revelation chapter 14.

This chapter has remarkable similarities to Revelation chapter 13. Firstly, the final world dictator, the Antichrist, is comparable to King Nebuchadnezzar, the first ruler of the sequence of world empires. Secondly, then as here a great image of the final world dictator will be made, which all men living will be required to worship. Thirdly, then as here true believers will refuse to bow to it, of whom many will die, but some will be delivered. From Daniel chapter 3 verse 25 they will be able to claim the presence of Christ at their side as they enter the fires of persecution. Finally, and very significantly, just as the image here was sixty cubits by six, so the number 666 is always associated with the number of the coming world dictator. It is the number of man, just short of seven, the divine and perfect number. Man's rebellion against God, which was here typified by Nebuchadnezzar's image, will continue throughout the Times of the Gentiles, and will appear fully developed in the end times in the 666 of the final Antichrist.

Note on the Aramaic Vocabulary of the Chapter

A few words should be said concerning the vocabulary used in this chapter, and in particular that used for the high officials of the Babylonian administration and the musical instruments which were played when the people were to bow down to the golden image. For scholarly unbelievers have tended to claim that the vocabulary used here supports a date for the book's composition later than the sixth century B.C. First, therefore, certain Persian words are used in the lists of administrative officials. Since Daniel clearly did not write his book before the Persian period had begun, it is to be expected that he would choose terms which would be best suited to be understood by the readers of his own day, the beginning of the Persian period. If the book had been written in Palestine during the Greek period, the second century B.C., as many liberal scholars claim, it would have been surprising if any Semitic-Babylonian words had been used at all. Secondly, certain of the musical instruments named in verse 5 are Greek. This is used as an argument for dating the composition of the book in the later Greek period. However, evidence mounts every year of scholarly investigation for the early cultural exchange between Greece and the Orient. Such an exchange of cultural artefacts is surely to be expected in Babylon's wide conquests and cosmopolitan court. So the evidence of the vocabulary used here supports a sixth century B.C. date for the composition of the

Book of Daniel, rather than a later second century date. Indeed, in this connection it is interesting to note that the Greek Septuagint translation of Daniel, which is known to have been composed in the second century B.C., has great difficulty in translating certain of the technical terms used in this chapter, which would be surprising if the book had been written in the same century. Rather, this fact supports an earlier date, and indicates that by the time the Septuagint was translated, certain older words had fallen out of use, and their meaning was not understood with certainty. Thus the divine inspiration of Scripture is confirmed again and the liberal critics are refuted.

CHAPTER 4

The Great King's Humiliation and Testimony

Chapter 4 contains Nebuchadnezzar's personal testimony to God. It is written by the great king himself mainly in the first person, and recounts how, through a second dream and its fulfilment in a serious illness, God humbled his pride and brought him to acknowledge the absolute sovereignty of the Most High God of heaven over all the kingdoms of men, and over himself also. It is a thrilling climax to the record of God's disciplinary, but gracious, dealings with him in the previous three chapters through the faithful witness of his loyal Jewish servants. Daniel was led to incorporate the record into his book for our great encouragement and God's own greater glory. Nothing is too hard for Him. We can expect to meet Nebuchadnezzar one day in the glory of heaven. Praise God for His grace!

1. The Introduction to Nebuchadnezzar's Testimony, vv.1-3

This chapter is unique among all the chapters of the Bible. For it written by the most powerful ruler of the world in Daniel's day, and comprises the great king's own worldwide proclamation of what God had done for him. Nebuchadnezzar, like all true converts to God, wishes the whole world to know what God has done for his soul. He here acknowledges, partly in poetical language, the greatness of God's wonders and signs, the eternity of His kingdom, and the enduring nature of His dominion, by contrast with the brevity of his own empire. The following chapter relates the remarkable story of how God dealt with him.

2. *Nebuchadnezzar's Account of his Second Dream, vv.4-18*

As with most of us, Nebuchadnezzar's root sin was pride. He could not be converted before God had dealt with that problem in his life. So God gave Nebuchadnezzar a second dream, which in symbolical language outlined what He was going to do to the king to humble him once and for all. During a period of his life when he was prospering peacefully and rather complacently in his regal surroundings, Nebuchadnezzar had another very disturbing dream, or rather nightmare. It so frightened him that he called for all his pagan wise men and asked them to interpret it for him, but, since the dream was from the true God, they with their occult practices were quite unable to help him. For some reason Daniel was not consulted first, but last of all. Perhaps Nebuchadnezzar suspected that the dream was bad news for himself, and that it did come from Daniel's God, but was reluctant to consult him, in case that was the truth. Was his conscience at work here? However, in his anxiety Nebuchadnezzar did turn to Daniel, and acknowledged his ability to reveal the mystery to him. He then, unlike previously in chapter 2, recounted the whole dream in great detail, before requesting an interpretation.

Nebuchadnezzar said that in his dream he saw a great and beautiful tree in the centre of the whole earth which grew tall and strong and provided shelter and food for all living things, including all mankind. Then he saw an angelic being, whom he called 'a watcher and a holy one', come down from heaven and command that the tree be chopped down, cut to pieces, and scattered. All those in the tree fled from it. But he saw that, strangely, the stump of the tree was left and bound with a metal hoop to prevent it from splitting, and then left to be watered by the dew. It was to be left among the beasts of the field. The tree was not completely destroyed; new growth could spring up from the roots and stump. But first 'seven times', which may mean seven years, were to elapse before this happened. In fact, in the account of the dream, the tree's restoration is not mentioned. Instead, an angelic watcher and holy one stated the purpose of the judgement on the tree, namely, that all peoples living might know that the Most High God rules supreme over all earthly kings, and sets up over the nations of the earth the basest of men. It is noticeable that in his account Nebuchadnezzar changed from the neuter pronoun to the masculine, as if he anticipated that this dream might concern a man, and probably himself. He had probably anticipated that it spelt some kind of disaster for himself, but wished Daniel to explain the judgement coming to him in detail. Note in the account the vital role of angelic beings, here uniquely called 'watchers and holy ones', who clearly superintend human affairs with a keen interest in maintaining God's glory. Angels appear later in the book in a similar role, especially in chapters 8-12. We little realise their power and place in God's government either of the world or of local churches; see also the Book of Revelation.

3. Daniel's Interpretation of the Dream, vv.19-27

Daniel understood the meaning of the dream at once, but was quite upset at the severity of God's predicted judgement on the great king, despite the latter's obvious pride. Daniel had undoubtedly grown quite fond of his earthly master, and was praying for his spiritual blessing rather than this judgement. So he hesitated a little before answering the king. But Nebuchadnezzar encouraged him to tell the whole matter to him clearly; so he did. Daniel explained that the tree represented the king in all his imperial greatness. Nebuchadnezzar was the most important man on earth in his day in the world's eyes. The decree passed by the heavenly court of watchers and holy ones was that of the Most High God Himself, who was going to drive Nebuchadnezzar from his throne into the fields like a wild animal. There he would behave like an ox and eat grass for seven times, or years, until he had learned his lesson concerning God's sovereignty in the world. Daniel reassured the king that his kingdom would be restored to him after he had humbled himself and recognised the sovereignty of God. Daniel proceeded therefore out of real affection for his master to warn Nebuchadnezzar to repent of his sins, to start to practise righteousness, and to show mercy to the poor of this world. If he did so, Daniel said that the king might be able to enjoy his prosperity a little longer than otherwise. God is always slow to judge, but swift to bless. His mercy triumphs over His judgement. But Daniel implied that eventually Nebuchadnezzar was to face a very humiliating experience from God's hand.

4. Nebuchadnezzar's Humiliating Illness, vv.28-33

About a year afterwards all this happened to Nebuchadnezzar. While he was in the act of proudly congratulating himself on all his magnificent achievements in building up Babylon to its then-present greatness, God spoke to him from heaven in the words of the dream, and announced the fulfilment of its judgement in every detail, until Nebuchadnezzar had acknowledged God fully. The great king was afflicted with a rare form of insanity, which made him behave like an ox and neglect himself throughout the next seven years. He was driven away from his palace, but Daniel probably saw to it that he was not mistreated by any of his subjects during his illness. He alone, perhaps, realised that there would be a happy outcome in time. Undoubtedly, Nebuchadnezzar owed a great deal to Daniel's faithful and consistent prayers. There certainly was no malice or retaliation against his earthly master for his sometimes unfair treatment of him. This is an example for us to follow.

Although secular history neither clearly confirms nor denies the occurrence of the king's illness, perhaps not surprisingly, it is interesting to note that a so-called 'Prayer of Nabonidus', which describes a similar illness in connection with Nabonidus, a later king of Babylon, has been found amongst the Dead Sea Scrolls. Perhaps this is a garbled account which really related to Nebuchadnezzar, rather than to Nabonidus. After all, the Book of Daniel can be taken as a reliable primary historical document in its own right.

5. *Nebuchadnezzar's Restoration and Conversion, vv.34-37*

At the end of seven long years of insanity Nebuchadnezzar's reason was restored to him when he looked up to heaven and acknowledged and gave glory to the Most High God. He had learned the hard way the essential lesson of humility before blessing which all of us find so hard to accept. He acknowledged the eternity of God's kingdom, the nothingness of men before God, and God's rightful and absolute sovereignty. Once he had done this, God gave him back his kingdom and regal honour and glory. Even his counsellors, probably influenced by Daniel, sought to re-establish his authority and respect in the kingdom. So in verse 37, in a humble, but dignified manner, Nebuchadnezzar praised God as the King of heaven, the righteousness of all God's deeds and ways, and acknowledged at last that He is able to humble all who walk in pride before God. He had been converted to God. Praise His Name! With God nothing is impossible; no-one is too hard for the Lord to save.

The Personal Application of the Chapter

The chief lesson of the chapter is that God both 'resists the proud' and 'gives grace to the humble'. We are nothing, and deserving of nothing, before Him; but, if we humble ourselves 'in the sight of the Lord', He will lift us up; see James 4.6, 10; and 1 Peter 5.6. Pride kept Nebuchadnezzar from salvation for a long time, but God dealt with him to humble that proud look of his, and eventually brought him into blessing untold. It must be so with our own naturally proud hearts. Before any person can be saved, he or she must humble themselves before God and acknowledge their deep sinfulness. Repentance of sin towards God must always precede faith in Jesus Christ for salvation. Any other message is a deficient gospel and will produce spurious results.

The Prophetic Significance of the Chapter

This incident seems to foreshadow some features of the last days, the period of Tribulation which will follow the Rapture of the Church of Christ. Nebuchadnezzar's seven years of insanity may foreshadow the seven years of Gentile insanity on earth during the Tribulation, when the last Satanically-energised king of Babylon the Great will be judged by God. Also, just as here an individual Gentile, represented by a tree that is felled and its stump preserved for future restoration, comes through God's judgement into the blessing of salvation, so in and through the judgements of the Tribulation many individual Gentiles will be saved and enter the millennial kingdom of Christ, as Revelation chapter 7 indicates. God's act of cutting down the proud Gentile tree and then restoring it will bring humility. During the coming kingdom of Christ the Gentiles will be blessed with and because of the Jews, but will be subject to them. Just as in chapter 3 we saw that God was 'able to deliver' the faithful Jewish remnant through the fires of Tribulation, so here we see that God is 'able to abase' all those who will walk in pride during that same time of judgement. Only, here it leads to their eternal blessing. The case is very different in the next chapter, to which we will now turn.

CHAPTER 5

Weighed in God's Balances and Found Wanting

In the chiastic subject structure of the Aramaic section of the book, chapter 5 corresponds to, and contrasts sharply with, chapter 4. If in chapter 4 the most famous king of Babylon, Nebuchadnezzar, was humbled by God, and eventually converted, in chapter 5 we see the downfall of the last king of Babylon, Belshazzar, who dies at the hands of the Medo-Persian invaders. Both proud kings were humbled by God, but one received salvation, while the other was lost eternally.

The date of the chapter is 539 B.C., the date of the end of the Babylonian Empire and the beginning of the Medo-Persian Empire. The Medes and Persians under Cyrus the Great had been besieging Babylon for some time, thus far without success; so strong were the city's walls and defences. Daniel had been living in comparative obscurity for some years, probably because his godly counsel was not sought by the later kings of Babylon, who had not followed Nebuchadnezzar's example in valuing his presence in the administration of the empire. In fact, according to chapters 7 and 8, Daniel had already received two further major visions from God concerning future events before this date, in the first and third years of Belshazzar's reign respectively. He was therefore even more prepared for the turn of events in this chapter than he had been before in chapter 4. This fact also indicates the non-chronological arrangement of parts of the book.

Many of the historical details of the chapter have been confirmed by scholarly investigations, including archaeological excavations on the site. The so-called 'Nabonidus Cylinder' has confirmed the existence of Belshazzar as co-regent with his father Nabonidus at this time, as mentioned in the Introduction. This chapter mentions 'the queen', who may have been the queen mother, and who calls Nebuchadnezzar the father of Belshazzar, rather than Nabonidus. There was probably a link by marriage between Nabonidus, Belshazzar, and Nebuchadnezzar through a daughter, or even a widow, of Nebuchadnezzar, although the precise situation is not clear. The details of the feast in this chapter correspond with what is known from history of Babylonian feasts, and even the hall in which it took place has probably been identified by archaeologists. The difficulty of the identity of 'Darius the Mede' has been mentioned in the Introduction also, but more than one solution is possible. So the critics have been confounded in their scepticism regarding the authenticity of the chapter.

1. Belshazzar's Blasphemous Feast, vv.1-4

While the armies of the Medes and Persians were surrounding Babylon, Belshazzar decided to hold a riotous party for his lords and ladies. Perhaps his philosophy of life was, 'Eat, drink, and be merry, for tomorrow we die'. At all events he completely disregarded the danger in which he and his subjects stood, perhaps because he falsely trusted in his security within the walls of Babylon. It is confirmed from historical sources that the Babylonian kings did hold very large parties for their aristocracy, so that the description of the party for a thousand of his lords is no exaggeration. Further, it has been discovered that it was the custom for the king to drink wine on a platform raised above the general level of the hall in which the party took place, so that it is also accurate to state that Belshazzar 'drank wine in front of the thousand'.

When Belshazzar had become somewhat inebriated by the wine, he took a fatal decision. He commanded that the vessels of gold from the Lord's Temple in Jerusalem be brought in, so that the company might drink from them. This was an act of gross blasphemy and sacrilege, which God could not, and did not, ignore. The whole drunken company indulged their carnal desires using the sacred vessels, probably the goblets used by the Jewish priests and Levites, for a thoroughly wrong purpose. The company even praised the goblets as if they were some of their own man-made gods. It was a gross sin which demanded immediate retribution.

2. The Writing on the Wall, vv.5-9
Scripture solemnly warns us all, 'Be not deceived. God is not mocked; for whatsoever a man soweth, that shall he also reap'; Galatians chapter 6 verse 7. Also, 'Pride goeth before destruction, and an haughty spirit before a fall'; Proverbs chapter 16 verse 18. Both of these Scriptures were fulfilled in the life of Belshazzar here. Let all unbelievers take note, and so avoid his sad fate.

No sooner had the king and his guests begun to desecrate the vessels of the Lord, than the fingers of a man's hand mysteriously appeared writing a cryptic message on the wall opposite them all. Frivolity changed at once to fear. Belshazzar was affected physically by his terror, so that his face changed colour and his knees began to knock together involuntarily. He obviously sensed a message of doom. As on previous occasions faced by Nebuchadnezzar, Belshazzar initially sought help from his occult diviners, astrologers, and so-called wise men, neglecting Daniel, the true prophet of God. The wise men could make nothing of the writing, and this fact alarmed Belshazzar even more than he had been before. Even his offer of gifts and the status of being the third ruler in the kingdom produced no satisfactory result. We have already referred in the Introduction to the fact that Belshazzar was at this time a co-regent with his father, Nabonidus, so that the reference to 'the third ruler', rather than the second, is entirely historically accurate.

3. The Queen's Intervention, vv.10-12

At this critical point the queen, or possibly the queen mother, who had not been present at the riotous party until now, came into the banqueting hall, perhaps on hearing the unusual consternation of the whole company. Probably because she was a somewhat older lady, she remembered Daniel and his ability to interpret dreams and visions to Nebuchadnezzar, here called Belshazzar's father, or grandfather by marriage. She knew that he could help Belshazzar, because she recognised that he was a man of God with special expertise in this area of understanding. Daniel's wisdom had been recognised by all the older generation of the Babylonian royal family. The queen, therefore, knowing that Daniel was the man for the moment, strongly advised Belshazzar to call for him. It would seem that after Nebuchadnezzar died in 562 B.C., Daniel had not been called upon to serve the succeeding kings of Babylon in the way he had previously helped Nebuchadnezzar. Probably, this was because of his godliness, which did not suit the succeeding royals. Evidently, Daniel was available in Babylon at short notice, but probably living in semi-retirement during this stage of his life. He would by now have been about 80 years old anyway. The queen was confident that Daniel would be able both to read the writing on the wall and to give the king its interpretation without delay.

4. The Recall of Daniel from Retirement, vv.13-16

So it came about that Daniel was recalled into royal service once again. This prepares us to accept that there may be periods in the lives of God's servants during which their services are not called upon as frequently as previously in their younger years. But it also indicates that we never know when God may suddenly call us again into His service later in life, perhaps even after we have reached advanced years. There is no real retirement in the Lord's service. There is always some good work that a Christian can do all throughout his or her life to the very end of it, as with Daniel here. After this moment Daniel was always in the forefront of politics in Babylon, and continued to exert a very necessary godly influence on the ruling monarchs.

Belshazzar probably knew of, even if he had not previously consulted, Daniel. To his credit, Belshazzar showed great respect for Daniel under these circumstances, and acknowledged his excellent godly spirit, understanding, and wisdom in interpreting his legal father Nebuchadnezzar's dreams. He frankly admitted that the wise men of Babylon had completely failed to make any interpretation of the writing on the wall, and offered Daniel the gifts and position previously offered to the former advisers, if he would interpret the message for him. But Belshazzar's change of heart towards Daniel came too late to save either his life or his soul. For him the die was already cast; his eternal doom was sealed by his act of sacrilege. It is possible to put oneself beyond the reach of God's mercy, so that we face only His final judgement. Readers, be warned by the example of Belshazzar!

5. Daniel's rebuke of Belshazzar, vv.17-23
Certainly the aged prophet and statesman did not mince his words to Belshazzar, but severely rebuked him for failing to pay any heed to the example of his father Nebuchadnezzar's humiliating chastening by God in a past generation. Belshazzar evidently knew all about God's dealings with Nebuchadnezzar's pride in the form of an illness which led to his temporary removal from the kingship, and how Nebuchadnezzar had eventually responded to it in due humility before the Most High God. Instead, Belshazzar had gone his own way, ignored this warning, and continued to act in arrogant pride against God to the point of committing this act of sacrilege against Him. He had failed to honour the God in whose hand his very breath was held. So Belshazzar had sealed his own doom, as do all who despise God and ignore His most obvious warnings. Daniel had no use for the king's gifts and rewards, but proceeded to announce Belshazzar's fate from the writing on the wall.

6. Daniel's Interpretation of the Writing, vv.24-29

The writing on the wall clearly contained a cryptic message which was not immediately capable of being interpreted without help from God Himself. It is unclear in what form the message was written; whether horizontally in lines, or whether perhaps it was written vertically in lines as a kind of anagram. There was certainly something mysterious about it. But Daniel forthwith proceeded to read and interpret the writing for all present to understand; to him there was no problem in understanding it, or what God was saying to them. The writing was written in the language of Babylon, Aramaic, and contained only consonants; Daniel supplied the vowels. The words that were written on the wall were as follows:-

MENE, MENE, TEKEL, UPHARSIN

Taking each in turn he then explained the meaning of the message. In fact, each part of the writing had a double meaning. First, MENE means 'numbered'. This meant that God had numbered the years and days of Belshazzar's kingdom. The repetition of MENE meant that God had finished his kingdom. His allotted time of privilege and responsibility in the kingdom had come to an end. Secondly, TEKEL meant 'weighed', that is, weighed in God's balances as the Judge of all. Daniel gave TEKEL a second meaning, changing the vowels to read TEKAL, which in Hebrew means 'to be light', that is, of insufficient weight to tip God's balances. Translating TEKAL into Aramaic, Daniel then stated that Belshazzar had been put on God's balances and found to be wanting, that is, to fall short of what God required of him. Belshazzar had had certain light and knowledge given him by God, but had failed to respond or live up to it. Consequently, thirdly, UPHARSIN, meaning 'divided', or 'divisions', signified the fact that his kingdom had been divided. Daniel used the singular form of the word in his interpretation, PERES. But again Daniel added a second interpretation of this part of the message. By supplying a different set of vowels for PERES he changed it to PERAS, which is the word for Persia. So the full message said that the Babylonian kingdom was about to fall to the Medes and Persians who were even then besieging the city.

The full message, using an English translation, therefore read as follows:-

NUMBERED, NUMBERED; WEIGHED, LIGHT; AND DIVISIONS, PERSIA

Interpreted with the dual meanings it signifies: The days of your kingdom are numbered and have run out. You have been weighed in God's balances and found wanting. The kingdom is to be divided between the Medes and the Persians.

What an indictment for anyone to receive from God! Yet Belshazzar had fully deserved it, since he had ignored the warning example of his father Nebuchadnezzar and committed gross sacrilege against God. His final hour had come, and he was ill-prepared for it. All he could do was to honour his promises to Daniel out of respect and leave the issues with his God. It was already too late for him to repent and mend his ways. Reader, once again, be warned! Do not provoke God to His face, or you will face imminent judgement.

7. Belshazzar's Death, vv.30-31
The sentence of God against Belshazzar and Babylon was executed that very same night, and Belshazzar was killed by the invading armies of the Medes and Persians. For they had found a way to enter the city unexpected by the complacent Babylonians. Some Greek historians say that they had diverted the course of the River Euphrates through the city, and marched in along the river-bed. So Cyrus the Great captured the capital of the Babylonian Empire, and the whole empire thus fell into his control. A certain 'Darius the Mede' became king of Babylon, probably subordinate to Cyrus the Great. Although unknown by this name in secular sources, he has been identified with the

Medo-Persian general Gubaru, who ruled Babylon for the next fourteen years. This would accord with the age of Darius the Mede, namely, sixty-two years, at the time of the conquest in October 539 B.C. Incidentally, this account of the combination of the Medes and Persians in the conquest and subsequent rule of the empire confirms that the Medo-Persian Empire was one empire, not two separate ones, as liberal scholars would like to claim. No, Scripture is accurate here, as everywhere else in the book, once all the facts are taken into consideration.

There is thus a very stark contrast between the ends of chapters 4 and 5, between the respective ends of Nebuchadnezzar and Belshazzar. Both were very proud men; both were humbled by God. But there the likeness stops; for Nebuchadnezzar acknowledged his sin, humbled himself before God, and was converted, while Belshazzar simply acquiesced in his sentence of doom and was killed without mercy or hope of salvation.

The Personal Challenge of the Chapter

We, too, are living in days of partying, blasphemy, and immorality while the signs of the approach of the judgements of the end times are clearly all around us, if we only have eyes to see them. We should not live simply for the sinful pleasures of the moment, like Belshazzar, but prepare to meet our God, as Belshazzar did that fateful night. The Lord Jesus said that in the days of the coming of the Son of Man, a reference to Himself, men and women would be carelessly pursuing all their normal pleasures and other activities without a thought of His intervention or His judgement, as in the days of Noah before the Flood, and would be suddenly and irrevocably overtaken by the Tribulation judgements and lost for ever. Reader, again, be warned by this chapter to repent before the day of opportunity to obtain salvation is gone. Do not blaspheme God, His interests, or His people like Belshazzar; for retribution will surely come swiftly and fatally when you least expect it!

<u>The Prophetic Significance of the Chapter</u>
Scripture indicates that the last days will be marked by indifference to God and a false sense of security before the seal judgements are opened one by one by Christ. Belshazzar foreshadows the pleasure-mad world of the end times unaware of the impending judgement of God. Just as Belshazzar, the last king of the Babylonians, was killed in the sacrilegious act of desecrating the Jewish Temple vessels, so the final king of Babylon the Great, the Antichrist/Beast/Man of Sin, will meet his end after defying God and setting up the image of himself in the rebuilt temple in Jerusalem to secure universal worship for himself; see Revelation chapters 13 and 17-19. The fall of Babylon in Old Testament times prefigures the final destruction of Babylon the Great in the closing days of the Great Tribulation; for there is a clear moral, spiritual, and historical link and likeness between the two cities.

CHAPTER 6

Daniel's Deliverance from the Lions' Den

In the overall subject arrangement of the Aramaic section of the Book of Daniel, that is, chapters 2-7, chapter 6 corresponds to chapter 3. For both chapters contain the account of the persecution of the faithful Jewish believers in Babylon by a proud heathen king who set himself up to be worshipped as if he were God. Also, in both chapters the one true God intervenes miraculously to protect and deliver His servants from all harm. Finally, both chapters end with the heathen king acknowledging God and giving Him the glory due to His Name. So there is a happy ending to both chapters, despite the malice of the different enemies of the true believers.

1. Daniel's Promotion under Darius, vv.1-2
Although he was now, in 539 B.C., over eighty years old, Daniel reached the pinnacle of his career under the new king of Babylon, Darius the Mede. For Darius, who was probably a subordinate of Cyrus the Persian emperor, organised the newly-conquered empire into 120 provincial regions, called satrapies, under three presidents, to whom the 120 satraps were accountable. Despite his age, Daniel was at once promoted to become one of these three presidents, and Darius was so pleased with him, recognising his excellent spirit and sterling character and integrity, that he intended to make Daniel the chief president over the whole empire. This was a great tribute to Daniel's testimony in the world of his day. Can the same be said of us in our much humbler spheres of responsibility and influence today? The New Testament epistles stress in connection with the recognition of local assembly overseers that

they 'must have a good report' from those who are outside the assembly in the world around them. 1 Timothy chapter 3 verse 7 gives as the reason for this qualification the danger of the overseers falling into disgrace and so bringing reproach on the whole assembly.

2. *The Plot of Daniel's envious Fellow-governors, vv.4-9*

While Daniel's promotion did not bring anyone else into difficulties, it did make him the object of his fellow-governors' bitter envy and the target of their malicious attack. His eminent position was actually fraught with mortal danger. For Daniel's colleagues decided to try to eliminate him once and for all. Perhaps Daniel was frustrating their own ambitions, since they were probably much younger men, and perhaps also he was showing up by comparison with his honest and industrious character their own somewhat dishonest ways. At all events, they first of all tried their utmost to find some ground for accusation in Daniel's conduct of his most responsible job, but in this they completely failed. How would we have stood up to such scrutiny? Eventually they realised that the only way to find fault with him was to complain about his strong religious faith in God. This in itself was an eloquent testimony to Daniel's most godly conduct. Their hatred of him is seen in the contemptuous way they referred to him as 'this Daniel'. They could not stand his clear testimony to God. So they decided to hatch a plot which would remove Daniel from amongst them.

The conspirators assembled together to the king in some pretended excitement and agitation to put a suggestion to him which would flatter his pride and make him think that his administrators were very pleased with his leadership. They used flattering language and gave Darius the false impression that all the presidents and satraps had been consulted concerning this proposal, including, by implication, Daniel, who was not, of course, present at the meeting. How mean and hypocritical the human heart is! The proposal was that Darius as king should make a decree that forbade anyone to pray or make a petition to any god or man except himself for thirty days, on pain of being thrown into the den of lions. This decree would be irrevocable according to the law of the Medes and Persians, which overrode even the king's wishes in that second world empire. Darius, proud man that he was, fell into the trap, and immediately signed the decree. So would Daniel also fall into the trap set for him, or decide to compromise his faith in the one true God?

3. Daniel's Uncompromising Consistency, vv.10-11
Daniel soon came to know about this iniquitous decree, but it had absolutely no effect on either his faith in God or his courage in the face of extreme danger. He did not vary his usual pattern of devotional life with God in prayer even for one day. He did not even compromise by concealing his devotional activities, but opened his windows towards his beloved city Jerusalem and prayed as usual three times daily, kneeling down on his knees even at eighty years of age, until he was spied on and discovered by the conspirators. How low men will stoop to try to destroy a godly servant of the Lord! How brightly does Daniel's consistent testimony shine out by comparison with their despicable behaviour!

4. The Apparent Success of the Plot against him, vv.12-18
Now that the conspirators had the evidence they needed, they again assembled in some agitation and excitement to interrupt Daniel's private devotions and report him to the king. Darius saw at once what he had been tricked into doing, and was most displeased with himself for having been deceived by his subordinates, but it was too late for him to save Daniel's life himself. The law of the Medes and Persians stood against him. This world kingdom was only made of silver, not the gold of absolute monarchy like that of Nebuchadnezzar. Darius had to concede to the arrest and execution of his most trusted and valued servant. What a conceited fool he had been! However, Darius had come to respect Daniel and Daniel's God so much that, before he consigned the aged man to the den of lions, he

expressed his very real conviction that Daniel's God, unlike himself, would deliver him. For Daniel's consistently godly conduct and sterling faith in his God, whom he served continually, had so impressed the heathen king that it had begun to create faith in Darius' heart too. May the Spirit of God be able to speak to others through our testimonies before them in the same way today!

5. God's Deliverance of Daniel from the Lions, vv.19-24
Darius, deservedly, spent a sleepless night worrying about Daniel's fate in the den of lions. Before it was fully light, he hurried to the den and cried out in a sad and anguished voice to Daniel, in case he was still alive. He had some faith, but as yet not very great faith. He acknowledged that Daniel's God was the living God, and enquired if He had been able to deliver His faithful servant. However, he need not have doubted. Daniel's voice came back loud, calm, and clear, wishing the king well and long life, and stating that God had sent His angel to shut the mouths of the lions in the den, so that they had not harmed him at all. Daniel knew the reason for this, his blameless conduct before God and the king. God had honoured one who had honoured Him. So Daniel was rescued from the den and found to be none the worse for his ordeal. Darius then turned in fury on the malicious conspirators and their families, sending them immediately into the same den of lions as Daniel had been put in. They did not even get to the bottom of the den before the lions had devoured them all. There was summary and severe, if well-deserved, justice in those times, even poetic justice!

6. Darius's Decree acknowledging God, vv.25-28
Much as Nebuchadnezzar had done earlier in chapters 3 and 4, Darius now issued another decree countering his previous one. Unlike the earlier one, which gave honour only to himself, this second one acknowledged and glorified God as the living God, the God of Daniel, and declared His saving power in delivering Daniel from the power of the lions. Again, what a remarkable

testimony Daniel had, and what a close relationship with his God! So a potential tragedy for Daniel became a triumph for God.

The last verse of the chapter refers again to the same phrase used so contemptuously by the conspirators concerning Daniel, namely, 'this Daniel'. It states that he 'prospered during the reign of Darius and the reign of Cyrus the Persian'. God had seen to it that His faithful servant was honoured in the very sphere where many had despised and rejected him. This is a little foretaste of the glory that will be Christ's one day after His rejection and crucifixion during His first coming in humiliation. For Jesus, the despised Nazarene, once called 'this man' in contempt, will reign over the whole earth in the millennial kingdom. And Christ is 'the God of Daniel', the Greater than Daniel and every other faithful servant of His.

Incidentally, the reference here to the two linked reigns of Darius and Cyrus the Persian probably supports the fact that the Medo-Persian Empire was a joint empire and the second world empire of chapter 2, not two separate empires following each other as the second and third empires of chapter 2. Also, it is less likely that the 'and' should be translated as 'even', meaning that Darius the Mede is just another name for Cyrus the Persian, as a few scholarly believers have suggested. More probably, Darius the Mede was appointed as the king of the province of Babylon in subordination to Cyrus the Persian, the supreme emperor of the second world empire.

The Practical Challenge of the Chapter
Would we be prepared to continue to worship God openly and consistently, if we knew that in doing so we would endanger our lives? Believers in some countries of the world do face this dilemma today. All Daniel had to do to avoid trouble was to shut his windows and worship in secret. But that would have been an evidence of lack of faith and courage. True discipleship today can be as costly as it was in Daniel's day. We must be

prepared to witness openly before men and quietly submit to the consequences, trusting in God to deliver us, if it is His will to do so. Secret disciples are often not true disciples at all. Nicodemus and Joseph of Arimathea did eventually confess Christ openly and risk the consequences. Open confession of Christ as Lord is required for true salvation and thereafter expected throughout the Christian life. Again, who will 'Dare to be a Daniel'?

The Prophetic Significance of the Chapter
The prophetic significance of chapter 6 is similar to that of chapter 3. It foreshadows the future days of the Great Tribulation, when the final Antichrist will set himself up as the only object of worship, as if he were God. Then there will be universal persecution of all true believers, and, while many will be martyred, some, including the 144,000 Jewish witnesses, will be preserved from all harm to enter Christ's millennial kingdom victoriously in their mortal bodies. In this respect also, chapter 6 is the exact counterpart of chapter 3. For here we see the deification of a man, Darius, just as Nebuchadnezzar sought universal worship in chapter 3. Since the sinful heart of man remains the same in every generation, history has repeated itself, and will culminate in the final rebellion of man against God in the worship of the Antichrist, who is simply Satan's puppet king. Reader, be warned; this is how all human history will soon end! On whose side are you? Satan's, or God's, like Daniel?

God's View of the Five Future World Kingdoms

Chapter 7, the end of the Aramaic section of Daniel, is clearly the exact counterpart of chapter 2, which is its beginning. The chiastic structure of this whole section of the book is thus very marked. But whereas in chapter 2 we see in the image dream of Nebuchadnezzar man's view of the four world empires that span the Times of the Gentiles until the coming of Christ's kingdom, in chapter 7 we see in Daniel's vision of the four wild animals God's view of those same four Gentile world empires. To Him they are just unclean and devouring wild beasts. This is God's estimate of human government, and has surely been proved true by history.

Both chapters 7 and 8 predate chapters 5 and 6, since Daniel's visions here were received in the first and third years of Belshazzar's reign respectively, or 553 and 551 B.C. This prepares us to expect to find a subject arrangement in the Aramaic section as a whole, which has been demonstrated as we have commented on chapters 2-7. There is divine design in this book of Scripture, as in every one of its books.

From this point onwards in the book there are four separate visions given to Daniel, namely, chapters 7 and 8, then chapter 9 verses 24-27 from the first year of Darius' rule over Babylon, that is, 539 B.C., and finally chapters 10.1 to 12.4, a very long vision from the third year of Cyrus, 536 B.C. The latter three visions are all written down in Hebrew, since they concern God's sovereign dealings with His people Israel through the hands of Gentile world kingdoms in the future. The vision given to him here in chapter 7 is thus a bridge between the Aramaic and the Hebrew sections of the book. It contains the most comprehensive and far-reaching panorama of future world history in the whole of the Old Testament, adding some details not included in the parallel vision in chapter 2. Its interpretation is therefore of crucial importance in understanding Biblical prophecy as a whole. While there are various unbelieving approaches to the chapter, the majority of conservative Premillennial interpreters are agreed about the detailed meaning of the prophecies contained in it.

It has been observed concerning these four visions given to Daniel that they would have given him and all his later Jewish readers a great assurance that, although his people Israel were to go through a long period of suffering at the hands of various Gentile kingdoms, nevertheless in the end they would be delivered from all their tribulations at the Second Coming of Christ and share in the blessings of His millennial kingdom. Daniel would in fact have received the two visions of chapters 7 and 8 before he was called in to face Belshazzar and announce to him his imminent fate at the hands of the Medes and Persians, and also before he had to face the lions' den in chapter 6. This would have given him complete assurance of deliverance at those critical and difficult times in his life; for he would have known what the ultimate outcome was going to be before he had to face these trials of faith.

So, in summary, it can be said that while chapters 1 to 6 of the Book of Daniel tell us *how* believers like Daniel and his three friends can stand alone against all their enemies around them in an alien atmosphere, chapters 7 to 12 of the book tell us *why* it was worthwhile to do so in the end. This is the real spiritual value of predictive prophecy; it gives a light of hope to those who are to pass through difficult circumstances and experiences at the hand of evil men by God's permissive will. God is in complete control of all future events, and will bring us through them to enjoy His ultimate blessing one day. What a great, good, and gracious God He is! The very detailed predictions of future history, somewhat tedious and difficult to follow though they are, do have an important purpose in God's plans for us His people today, as well as for Israel in Old Testament days. Truly, 'God is still on the throne, and He will remember His own'! So we may be encouraged to remain resolute in our stand for God today in a wicked world just as Daniel and his friends did in their day; for we are on the victory side!

1. Daniel's Vision of the Four Wild Beasts, vv.1-8

God granted Daniel this 'dream and visions' as he lay in bed one night asleep very early in the reign of the last evil Babylonian king Belshazzar. Daniel recorded the dream-vision in writing, and related to us the following summary of it. He first saw the four winds of heaven stirring up the waters of the great sea. Now 'the Great Sea' in Scripture does sometimes describe the Mediterranean Sea, and it may do so here, but some interpreters understand the great sea here to represent the nations in restless tumult. The four winds probably symbolise God's sovereign and universal authority clashing with the plans of rebellious mankind. A great conflict is in progress throughout the whole of the Times of the Gentiles surveyed in the ensuing vision. Four great wild animals emerged from the tumult of the sea in succession, each quite different from the other three. What a horrific sight man's rule of the earth is in God's view of him! Natural man is untamed and very cruel, not even worth describing by the precious metals of the dream of chapter 2. Believing Premillennial interpreters of this passage are agreed concerning the meaning of the four wild beasts. The latter represent the same four successive world empires as are found in chapter 2, namely, Babylon, Medo-Persia, Greece, and Rome.

The First Beast (Babylon), v.4

The first beast which Daniel saw in his vision undoubtedly represents the Babylonian Empire headed by its most successful emperor, Nebuchadnezzar. It is here represented by a lion, the king of beasts, but with the wings of the king of birds, the eagle. It is remarkable that the gates of ancient Babylon were guarded by statues of winged lions similar to this symbol of the Babylonian Empire. The reference to the wings being plucked off and the lion being made to stand on two feet like a man, and its being given the mind of a man, probably refers to God's affliction of Nebuchadnezzar with a rare form of insanity described in chapter 4, which illness was a punishment for his pride and led directly to his conversion.

The Second Beast (Medo-Persia), v.5

The second beast to emerge from the great sea resembled a bear raised up on one side. This clearly represents the Medo-Persian Empire, in which the Persians were for the most part the dominant rulers. Liberal and unbelieving attempts to maintain that there was a separate Median Empire before the Persian Empire are contradicted by the historical evidence. Cyrus the Persian entered the conquered city of Babylon very shortly after Darius the Mede took it; the latter king was probably subordinate to Cyrus, but ruling there at the same time as Cyrus. It was thus a joint empire with a dominant partner. This situation is envisaged in the bear being raised up on one side. The combination of the Medes and the Persians in the empire's rule and legal system is mentioned in chapter 6 verses 8, 12, and 15. Then in chapter 8 verse 20 the ram with its two horns of unequal length is identified definitely as 'the kings of Media and Persia', confirming the matter. The symbolism of the bear suggests that, while the empire would be powerful and ferocious, it would lack the kingly authority and majesty of the Babylonian Empire, being instead somewhat heavy and clumsy. The three ribs in the bear's mouth clearly represent subject peoples within the Medo-Persian Empire, possibly Babylon, Lydia, and Egypt, but this is uncertain. Jerome (ca. A.D. 340-420), the Latin church father and translator of the Vulgate, suggested in his commentary on Daniel that they were the heartlands of the empire themselves, Media, Persia, and

Babylon. The fact that the bear was told to arise and devour much flesh after it was seen with three ribs already in its mouth tends to support Jerome's view. The conquest of other countries was to follow the initial consolidation of the empire. At all events, this view of the Medo-Persian Empire tallies with the known history of the empire from 539 to 336 B.C. It was strong, but cruel.

The Third Beast (Greece), v.6

According to the view taken in this study, the third wild beast represents the Greek Empire of Alexander the Great, which rapidly, like a leopard, overran the Persian Empire after 336 B.C. The four wings of a bird on the back of the leopard suggest the lightning-like character of Alexander's conquests. Attempts by unbelieving liberal scholars to prove that the third empire is that of Persia are quite unconvincing, as explained in the foregoing section on the second empire. The known facts of history just do not support this interpretation, but rather the Premillennial one, that it is Greece. This beast's four heads clearly correspond to the four Greek generals who divided up Alexander's dominions between themselves after his sudden death in 323 B.C. at the height of his success. These four generals were: first, Lysimachus, who controlled Thrace and Bithynia; secondly, Cassander, who controlled Macedonia and Greece; thirdly, Seleucus, who controlled Syria, Babylonia, and territories to the east as far as India; and fourthly, Ptolemy, who controlled Egypt, Palestine, and Arabia Petrea. The prediction thus perfectly fits known Greek history. The Greek generals and their successors ruled these territories until the rising Roman Empire gradually dislodged them during the succeeding centuries.

The Fourth Beast (Rome), vv.7-8

It is of crucial importance to understand that the fourth beast represents, not Greece, but Rome. The Roman Empire was established quite gradually, rather than suddenly like the Greek Empire of Alexander, over more than one century, and was much more ruthless in its subjugation of its subject peoples than all the preceding empires. In this important respect it was quite different from all of these empires, as verse 7 states. Before the final phrase of the verse, 'and it had ten horns', must be understood the well-known 'prophetic gap' of Old Testament prophecy, which never includes predictions of the New Testament Church age. The ten horns here refer to the ten kings of the yet future phase of the Revived Roman Empire. In chapter 2 these ten kings were represented by the ten toes of Nebuchadnezzar's image. Here in chapter 7 much more detail is given of the leader and history of that future form of the Roman Empire than chapter 2 gives. In particular, we are introduced to a person called the 'little horn', who starts his career as just one horn among the ten horns, but then plucks up three of his fellow-horns by the roots, and becomes the leader of all ten. This person, who is to be identified with the first Beast of Revelation chapter 13, the Man of Sin of 2 Thessalonians chapter 2, and the Roman Prince of Daniel chapter 9 verses 26-27, speaks great words of blasphemy against God and seeks to usurp the worship of mankind from God to himself.

2. *The Ancient of Days judges the Four Wild Beasts, vv.9-12*
Daniel now sees an awesome vision of the Eternal God depicted as 'the Ancient of Days' judging both the fourth beast and his empire. The first phrase of verse 9 should be translated, 'I beheld until thrones were set up'. This is the establishment of the judgement, not the casting down of the thrones. 'The Ancient of Days' here is distinguished from the 'Son of Man' of verse 13, who comes into the Presence of 'the Ancient of Days'. The latter title must therefore here refer to God the Father in His purity, eternity, holiness, and righteous judgement. In Revelation chapter 1 some of these features of 'the Ancient of Days' are used to describe the risen Lord Jesus Christ in His judge character as the Son of Man. They confirm the Deity of Christ. Here God's throne was like a fiery flame in its holiness and judgement of sin. The reference to the wheels of God's throne reminds us of Ezekiel's vision of God's throne in chapter

1 of his prophecy. These turned every way to execute His judgements in the earth. A fiery stream of holy judgements issued forth from Him. Myriads of holy angels were standing before God's throne serving Him. The other thrones would be for redeemed saints and angels, who assist God in His judgement.

Then books containing the records of the deeds of men were opened as the judgement was set up. The great and impressive words which the little horn had spoken in blasphemy against God were taken into account for judgement, and the result was, as Daniel saw in his vision, that the fourth beast, represented by its final ruler, the little horn, was killed and its body destroyed by fire. We know from Revelation chapter 19 that this will be the fate of the Beast and the False Prophet, his henchman, at the battle of Armageddon. They will be the first occupants of the lake of fire. This will be the sudden end of the fourth beast and his empire. The three preceding empires certainly had their dominions taken from them by the empires which followed them, but some aspects of their civilisations were continued in the realms of the empires which had conquered them until the whole period of the Times of the Gentiles had run its course. The latter period will end at the Second Coming of Christ.

3. The Son of Man receives the Fifth World Kingdom, vv.13-14
The Lord Jesus Christ clearly identified Himself with the Son of Man mentioned in this vision. In the Gospel records He often took upon His lips this description of Himself, beginning with Matthew chapter 8 verse 20. It is a Messianic title, not a reference to mankind in general, nor even the nation of Israel, as some liberal scholars have thought. His coming into the Presence of the Ancient of Days with the clouds of heaven indicates His own Deity. The time in view is Christ's Second Coming in glory to the earth. Then He will at last receive His rightful due, which He was denied at His first coming in grace, namely, the dominion and glory of the whole world. This will be the fifth and final kingdom to be established in the earth, and it will last

for ever, never to be destroyed or superseded like the previous four kingdoms. God Himself in the person of His Son, the Messiah, will intervene to establish it. It will not be established in any other way.

4. *The Angel's Interpretation of the Vision, vv.15-27*
Daniel was deeply affected by his visions, and very troubled about them. He did not yet understand what they meant. So he asked one of the attending angels to explain the visions to him. The angel certainly understood their meaning, and was willing to convey it to God's beloved servant. This tells us that the rightful inhabitants of heaven understand much of God's purposes even now. We underestimate the knowledge and power of angels to our loss.

Summary Interpretation of the Vision, vv.15-18
The angel's initial explanation of the visions was very brief. The four great beasts represented four different kings who would one day arise in the world. But in the end the saints of the Most High God would receive the kingship of the earth, and hold it for ever. Thus even from this summary interpretation we learn that believers will reign with Christ in His future eternal kingdom.

Daniel's Enquiry concerning the Fourth Beast, vv.19-22
Daniel was not really satisfied with this brief explanation. He wanted to understand the truth and significance of the fourth beast and its little horn. It seemed to him so very different from the other three beasts and so dreadful in its import. Surely terrible times were ahead for the world and his own people, Israel. In this he was perfectly correct. He had seen in his vision that the little horn not only spoke great blasphemous words, but made war against the saints and even overcame them, until the Ancient of Days intervened, judged in their favour, and gave them the kingdom. What would it all mean for believers?

Note that in these verses Daniel adds a few details concerning the fourth beast which have not been mentioned so far in his record of the vision, namely, the beast's teeth of iron, probably speaking of its cruelty, and its nails of brass, which perhaps describe its ferocity. The angel who gave the explanation of verses 17-18 had already introduced the subject of the saints of the Most High God for the first time in this vision. Now Daniel expands a little on it and seeks a fuller explanation.

The Angel's Reply to Daniel, vv.23-27
Accordingly, the angel who was attending Daniel elaborated on the subjects of the fourth beast, its ten horns, the little horn, and his war against the saints. All concerned with the vision recognised that it emphasised these aspects of the revelation more than it did all the three preceding beasts with their empires. The fourth beast with his empire would be different from those which had preceded it in that it would be truly worldwide in its sway, treading down and breaking in pieces those other kingdoms.

Now the old Roman Empire was not worldwide, just the greatest empire until that time. This ten horn phase of the kingdom must therefore be still future to our own day, because nothing exactly like it has yet arisen in the world. Premillennial interpreters of Scripture believe that it will not be formed in its fullness before the New Testament Church has been translated to heaven by Christ's coming to the air for her. They understand a gap in the record of the prophecy corresponding to the Church age, the Age of God's Grace. Precursors of the ten horns appear to be arising in our own day in the reformation of the old Roman Empire within the expanding boundaries of the European Union, but this is only a precursor of the empire in its final form, which will probably involve considerable expansion and realignment of national boundaries after the Rapture of the true Church has occurred.

The ten horns represent ten kings who hold power simultaneously, but another horn, an eleventh, will arise after they have, displace three of the ten kings, and assume control of the whole empire. This is clearly, again, the first Beast of Revelation chapter 13, who demands worldwide worship as God, speaking blasphemously against the One True God. He it is who will wage a war of attrition against the believers of those days, and will appear for a time to succeed in his aims, killing many of them according to Revelation chapter 13. He will also attempt to change the times of religious observances and religious traditions which honour God in favour of the worship of himself, the deification of man, and Satan's man at that.

Now in verse 25 we have introduced into the interpretation the first occurrence in Scripture of the time-period during which the Beast, the Man of Sin, or the coming Roman Prince will be allowed to succeed in his evil designs, namely, 'a time and times and the dividing of time'. This is usually taken to refer to the last three and a half years of the future Great Tribulation, which is so often referred to in the Book of Revelation later, either in that form, or as forty-two months, or as 1260 days. A prophetic year is thus to be understood as 360 days, rather than a solar year. So the Beast will be limited by God's sovereign appointment in what he can do to the believers of those days; their ordeal will not last longer than three and a half years. Then, according to verse 26, God will intervene in judgement, take the Beast's kingdom away from him, destroy it, and replace it with the worldwide kingdom of Christ. The believers of those days will at last be vindicated by God at Christ's appearing in glory and receive authority to rule with and for Christ in His millennial kingdom. Christ will reign for ever, and all will serve and obey Him. Note that the reference here to the Most High ruling must be understood to refer to Christ's rule as the Messianic Son of Man of verses 13-14. Thus Christ is identified with the Most High God.

5. *The Effect of the Vision on Daniel, v.28*
Daniel was overwhelmed by the far-reaching significance and gravity of the vision which he had been allowed to see, and it had an adverse physical effect upon him. But at the time he

kept quiet about what he had seen, until, that is, the time came for him to write this book in which the vision is recorded for us all to understand and profit from. He was a specially favoured servant of the Lord, privileged to see things that few others have ever seen. In part, this was evidence of God's sovereign choice; but also Daniel by his steadfast faithfulness had proved himself a worthy vessel of testimony for the Lord his God. May we prove ourselves the same as he!

CHAPTER 8

The Vision of the Ram, the He Goat, and the King of Fierce Countenance

So ends the Aramaic section of the Book of Daniel, which has extended from chapter 2 verse 4 to the end of chapter 7, about half of the whole book. It has largely concerned the Times of the Gentiles, their world kingdoms, and their fate at the coming of Christ to rule in His millennial kingdom. Now Daniel reverts to writing in Hebrew, the language of his own then-exiled people, the Jews. And the remaining three major visions largely concern God's dealings with His people Israel through the days of the Gentile kingdoms. Hard times of trial and discipline lay ahead for them, but in the end God would always deliver them, principally at the Second Coming of Christ to reign.

Chapter 7, then, was a bridge chapter, which summarised the Times of the Gentiles from God's point of view, and concentrated attention on the climactic events relating to the fourth world empire which will culminate in the Second Coming of Christ. Now Daniel's second major vision in chapter 8 concerns the empires of Persia and Greece as they relate to Israel. Here both Persia and Greece are named, just as Babylon was named in chapter 2. Daniel chapter 9 includes the prophetic vision of Israel's history from the time of Ezra and Nehemiah until the Second Coming of Christ, during which period they will encounter much trouble, especially in the last years before Christ returns. The final long vision in chapters 10-12 predicts in great detail the history of the wars of the Persian and Grecian kings over the land of Israel, with the final part predicting the end of the age, the period of the Revived Roman Empire, the campaign of Armageddon, as it is called in the Book of Revelation, and the deliverance of Israel at Christ's coming to reign.

1. The Circumstances of the Vision, vv.1-2

Daniel's second vision was given to him in the third year of Belshazzar, the last king of Babylon, that is, in 551 B.C., or a full twelve years before the final fall of the Babylonian Empire and Belshazzar's death. This has been confirmed by the contemporary historical records contained in *The Babylonian Chronicle*, the principal reliable source for this period. So the events of chapter 8 did not take place immediately before those of chapter 5, but some time before then. This fact makes the clear predictions of the chapter the more remarkable. Although Daniel was apparently awake when he first received this vision, he was transported in spirit to Susa, or Shushan, the capital of the later Persian Empire, some two hundred miles to the east of Babylon. He was thus projected into the whole environment of the future Persian and Greek empires to receive the message of the vision. The palace, or royal residence, of Shushan was situated in the province of Elam. At the time when Daniel had this vision Elam was probably not a province of Babylon, but it certainly became the centre of the later Persian Empire. The whole description of the circumstances of the vision thus accords with the events concerning the future times which are predicted in it. In fact, Daniel found himself in spirit beside the Ulai canal.

2. The Great Ram, vv.3-4

As soon as Daniel became conscious of his circumstances, he saw a ram standing on the bank of the canal. It had two high horns, but one of the horns, the one that grew up last, was higher than the other. Now in verse 20 the ram is interpreted to represent the kings of Media and Persia. This explains the symbolism perfectly; for the kingdom of Media was the earlier of the two kingdoms to rise to power, but it was not as powerful as the kingdom of Persia which rose to power a little later than Media. And the vision serves to confirm that Media and Persia formed a joint empire, the second world empire, not two separate empires, as liberal scholars often claim. The ram then charged irresistibly westwards, northwards, and southwards wherever he pleased to extend his empire, until he became great. This accords with the history of the Medo-Persian Empire, which conquered Babylon and Palestine to the west of its capital, Asia Minor to the north, and Egypt to the south.

3. The He Goat from the West, vv.5-7

While Daniel was pondering the meaning of this part of the vision, he saw a he goat come very swiftly from the west across the whole earth and viciously attack the ram with the two horns using its own one conspicuous horn, which was situated between its eyes. The he goat was obviously very angry with the ram, and this was probably the reason why he attacked him. The ram could not resist the powerful assault of the he goat, and his two horns were broken. Not content with this, the he goat proceeded to throw the ram to the ground and trample on him. In the light of the interpretation of verse 21 that the he goat represents the king of Greece, this scenario becomes quite clear. For the kings of Greece were enraged with the kings of Persia for invading their land some years before this, and Alexander the Great attacked the Persians in retaliation for their earlier aggression against the mainland of Greece. Alexander's smaller, but more efficient, army completely overwhelmed the Persian forces in three major battles at the Granicus River in 334 B.C., at Issus in 333 B.C., and at Gaugamela near Nineveh in 331 B.C. So Alexander succeeded the Persians, and became the emperor of the third world empire.

4. The Great Horn broken and succeeded by Four Horns, v.8

When the he goat was at the height of his power, his great horn was suddenly broken, and in its place grew up four conspicuous horns covering the four points of the compass. The interpretation confirms the later fact of history, that Alexander the Great died very suddenly at the age of nearly thirty-three, and his empire was divided between his four chief generals, Cassander, Lysimachus, Seleucus, and Ptolemy, who each assumed control of a different area of Alexander's empire, as mentioned in the commentary on chapter 2. But none of them had the same strength as Alexander had wielded. All this lay in the distant future in Daniel's day, so that Alexander, if he had had access to, and understood, the writings of the Hebrew prophets, could have been warned of his untimely death before it happened. Sadly, he appears not to have been prepared for eternity.

5. *The Little Horn out of the Kingdom of Greece and his Evil Career, vv.9-14*

Daniel saw that out of one of the four kingdoms comprising the Greek Empire emerged a little horn, which proceeded to grow very great towards the south, the east, and 'the pleasant land' (literally 'the beautiful', with the word 'land' understood), by which is meant Palestine, or Canaan, which lay between Syria and Egypt. Secular history documents these conquests as those of Antiochus Epiphanes, the eighth king in the Syrian dynasty, who ruled from 175-164 B.C. and has left an indelible mark on all subsequent history by his outrageous actions. Much of the history of his reign is recorded in the Apocryphal Books of Maccabees. So accurate is the prophecy in Daniel that many scholarly unbelievers have thought that it could not be prophecy dating from the sixth century B.C., but history written by another later writer in the second century B.C. But there is no difficulty to faith to accept that God both predicts and controls the future completely, so that this is understood to be pure prophecy which has now been fully fulfilled.

In verse 10 Antiochus is said to have grown so great that he reached 'the host of heaven' and cast some of 'the host' and 'the stars' to the ground and trampled on them. This is best understood to refer to his persecution and destruction of some of the Jews, the people of God, and his defiance of the angelic hosts who protect them. Certainly, he blasphemed God and all heavenly powers in his career of persecution. He set out to deify himself, thus defying God as 'the Prince of the host' of Israel. His pretensions were similar to those of 'the little horn' of chapter 7 verses 8 and 20, although that horn grew out of the fourth world empire, not the third, as here. Antiochus stopped the Jews offering their daily sacrifices and desecrated the Jewish sanctuary so badly that it had to be completely destroyed and renovated by the Maccabees. Verse 12 states that this little horn, Antiochus, would have the host, the Jewish people, given over to him, 'because of transgression', which may mean either 'because of the Jews' transgressions', or 'in Antiochus' act of rebellion against God'. Either way, the result was that Antiochus 'cast down the truth to the ground', that is, the true worship of God through the Mosaic Law, and for a time appeared to get away with his sacrilege and to prosper through it.

In verse 13 Daniel heard a holy angel asking another holy angel how long this scenario of sacrilege was going to be allowed to go on for. For God will not be mocked and defied for ever, and the inhabitants of heaven well know that. The answer in verse 14 is that this state of things would last 2,300 'evenings and mornings', or 2,300 full days; see Genesis 1. These are literal twenty-four hour days, not years, as the Seventh Day Adventists have mistakenly understood them to be. The latter cult expected Christ to come in 1884 on this false basis, but in this they were proved wrong. No, the fulfilment has already occurred in the days of Antiochus Epiphanes, whose entire period of abominations committed against God lasted from 171 to 165 B.C., exactly 2,300 days. Although this period does not correspond with the whole period of the yet future seven-year Tribulation period, it nevertheless foreshadows it. Antiochus Epiphanes was a precursor of the Man of Sin, who will do similar things to the people of God and set himself up as God in the rebuilt Jewish temple. Antiochus met his end providentially by a horrible disease in 164 B.C. The Beast/the Man of Sin will meet his fate at the Battle of Armageddon, according to Revelation chapter 19. After this, in both cases, the sanctuary would be cleansed and restored to its rightful state and use.

6. Daniel's Introduction to Gabriel, the Interpreter of the Vision, vv.15-19

Daniel very much wished to understand the meaning of this vision, particularly as it appeared to relate to his own people, Israel, and their evidently troubled future, but could not do so unaided. At this point there appeared to him the angel Gabriel in the form of a man, as often is the case with angelic beings in Scripture. A man's voice called Daniel's attention to this mighty angel between the banks of the Ulai canal. The voice, which may have been that of God Himself, instructed Gabriel to explain to Daniel the meaning of the vision. Gabriel thus appears as God's special messenger for the first time in Scripture; he appears again in chapter 9 to Daniel, then not until just prior to the births of John the Baptist and the Lord Jesus to Zacharias and Mary respectively in Luke chapter 1. This fact denoted the importance of both the occasion and the message conveyed here. God does not send His servants on unnecessary or unimportant missions.

Daniel was afraid in the presence of such an august servant of God. But Gabriel kindly explained that the ultimate meaning of the vision concerned, not his own day, but 'the time of the end'. Upon hearing this, Daniel fell into a deep sleep with his face to the ground. Gabriel, however, roused him and made him stand up and continue listening to him. He explained that the vision concerned 'the latter end of the indignation', or 'the appointed time of the end'. 'The indignation' must refer to the future Great Tribulation, which is described in various ways in different parts of Scripture, and this is the usual meaning of 'the time of the end' also; see chapter 11 verse 40.

Now since the vision so far has clearly referred in the first instance to the times of Antiochus Epiphanes, rather than to the yet future Tribulation, and has been demonstrated to have been fulfilled already, there is a problem in understanding Gabriel's words here. The matter is only resolved when we understand that the subsequent interpretation of the vision in its ultimate meaning and reference goes beyond the reference of Daniel's previous record of it. The previous record, fulfilled by Antiochus Epiphanes to the letter already, foreshadows a still darker scene in the days of the yet future Tribulation, when another ruler, like Antiochus, but worse than he was, will appear for a time on the world stage. There is sometimes this climactic character in Biblical prophecy, one prophecy foreshadowing another similar prophecy concerning later times. Both God and His adversary, Satan, are working to a predetermined or determined plan throughout history, so that similar events and people recur at various times.

7. The Interpretation and its Reference to 'A King of Fierce Countenance', vv.20-26

To embark on Gabriel's interpretation of the vision, therefore, we note, first of all, that in verses 20-23 he interprets the visions of the ram and the he goat in exactly the same way as we have already done earlier in this chapter, where we used the identifications given here. The two-horned ram represents the kings of Media and Persia. The he goat represents the king of Greece. Its great horn represents its first king, Alexander the Great. The four horns represent the four kingdoms of his generals, as explained earlier.

Then Gabriel continues by saying that 'in the latter time of their kingdom', when wicked men have reached the height of their transgressions against God, 'a king of fierce countenance' will arise. From the note of the time when he is expected to appear, namely, 'the time of the end', and from a few things that are said about him, it would appear that Gabriel is not here primarily referring to Antiochus Epiphanes, but to a future ruler who will come to the forefront of history in the Tribulation period, of whom Antiochus was just a foreshadowing. This has been disputed, but most scholarly believers do accept that 'the king of fierce countenance' has not yet appeared on the world stage. What they have not been certain or unanimous about, however, has been his precise identity.

There have been four main views of the matter held by reputable Bible teachers. We shall present all four views here, with the writer's preferred view indicated, but not insisted upon. First, then, as we have already indicated, there is the view that these verses have already been fulfilled by Antiochus Epiphanes. Certainly, there are some clear correspondences between him and this 'king of fierce countenance'. But there are a few points of difference also. First of all, there is the repeated mention of 'the time of the end' in verses 17, 19, 23, and 26, which was not true of the days of Antiochus. Secondly, Antiochus did not exactly attack 'the Prince of princes', Christ, although he set himself up as God. This attack must refer to Armageddon in Revelation chapter 19. Thirdly, this king seems to be involved with things occult and directly Satanic, understanding 'dark sentences', which appears to go a little beyond Antiochus and to point to an evil character of the end times. Fourthly, although the Lord Jesus referred to an 'abomination of desolation' which was similar to that committed in the Temple sanctuary by Antiochus, He spoke of this act as still future to His day, in fact, as the signal for the start of the Great Tribulation; see Matthew chapter 24 and Mark chapter 13.

The second view which has been held concerning this king is probably the predominant one among Premillennial Bible scholars, namely, that he is to be identified with the first Beast of Revelation chapter 13, the little horn of Daniel chapter 7, the Roman Prince of Daniel chapter 9, the wilful king of Daniel chapter 11, the idol shepherd of Zechariah chapter 11, the Man of Sin of 2 Thessalonians chapter 2, and the Antichrist of 1 John chapter 2. In other words, these scholars think that all these Scriptures refer to the same person. This has the merit of simplicity and consistency of interpretation. According to this view, the second Beast of Revelation chapter 13 is quite subordinate to this first Beast, and only referred to in that Scripture.

However, the third view is that some of the above Scriptures and this reference in Daniel chapter 8 to 'the king of fierce countenance' refer not to the first Beast of Revelation chapter 13, but to the second Beast mentioned there. Such scholars identify the wilful king of Daniel chapter 11, the idol shepherd of Zechariah chapter 11, and the Antichrist of 1 John chapter 2 with the second Beast rather than the first, on the ground that the latter must be an apostate Jew rather than a Gentile, since he arises from 'the land' (of Israel), not the sea of Gentile nations. Certainly, the second Beast of Revelation chapter 13 must be a Jew, but it is an unresolved question whether, or not, the first Beast is a Gentile or an apostate Jew. Even as the Roman Prince of Daniel chapter 9 he could be a Jew originating from within the confines of the Revived Roman Empire, so that both Beasts may prove to be apostate Jews. The question must be asked whether the Jewish nation would ever accept as their false Messiah anyone who was not in some way part of their own nation? When all the evidence in each relevant passage is examined, the matter is still unclear to us. We await the event to receive the final answer to these questions.

The fourth view is a little different from the foregoing views, but deserves at least some consideration. It is that 'the king of fierce countenance' is to be identified with 'the king of the north' of chapter 11 and the latter-day 'Assyrian' persecutor of Israel mentioned in Isaiah and Micah. Scholars who hold this view point out that this fierce king originates from within the Grecian kingdom of Syria, rather than the Revived Roman Empire. They hold that the little horn of chapter 7 is different from the little horn here in chapter 8, not another reference to the same man. This view has implications for the translation and interpretation of the war of the end times mentioned in Daniel 11 verses 40 onwards. These scholars understand the chief subject throughout that section to switch from the wilful king at the beginning of the passage to the king of the north towards its end. We shall consider the likelihood, or otherwise, of this view when we comment on chapter 11. Suffice it to say, that some scholars who hold this view relate the first Beast's 'deadly wound' of Revelation chapter 13 directly to military action by the king of the north, the invasion of the latter-day Assyrian, and the invasion by Gog and Magog of Ezekiel chapters 38-39. They would see this as taking place at the mid-point of the Tribulation and being the reason for its turning-point. They think that the divine removal of the king of the north at the end of Daniel chapter 11, if it really does refer to this character rather than to the wilful king, will provide the first Beast with his opportunity to assume world control in a way he had not before his deadly wound was miraculously healed by Satanic power. This is certainly one possible way of correlating all these relevant Scriptures, but it is not certain that it is the only, or perhaps the most likely, way of doing so. The second view explained above remains the simplest and perhaps the most convincing view, namely, that all these various Scriptures relate to the same man, the first Beast of Revelation chapter 13.

At all events, this king of fierce countenance will persecute the people of God in his day, as is predicted of the first Beast in Revelation chapter 13, and for a time will prevail over them. But when he opposes Christ Himself at His Second Coming, he will be destroyed by Christ supernaturally, as Revelation chapter 19 predicts will happen to both Beasts.

This interpretation of the vision may be regarded as an illustration of a double fulfilment of prophecy, in that Antiochus Epiphanes is used as a type and foreshadowing of the ultimate king who will persecute the people of God in the days of the Great Tribulation.

8. Daniel is appalled by the Vision and becomes ill, v.27
Daniel was so distressed to learn of the sufferings which his

people were to endure in the future that he became ill, and had to take some time off from his work for the king. Although he soon made himself return to his duties for the Babylonian king, he remained profoundly disturbed by his vision, which he still did not fully understand. He was learning that only the future Persian kings amongst the kings of the coming world empires would behave relatively kindly towards his people Israel. Other kings would trample Jerusalem under their feet throughout the Times of the Gentiles. As we shall learn from chapter 9, such was the price of Israel's serious sins against the Lord their God. But chapter 9 will also point the way forward to Israel's eventual restoration.

Daniel's Prayer and God's Prophecy of Israel's Seventy Weeks Discipline

We come now to the chapter which includes Daniel's third vision concerning his people Israel in the future. It is one of the most remarkable chapters in the Bible, both because of the deep spirituality of Daniel's prayer with which it commences, and also because of the panoramic nature of the revelation concerning Israel's future given to him in answer to his prayer. It is no exaggeration to say that 'because of the comprehensive and structural nature of Daniel's prophecies, both for the Gentiles and for Israel, the study of Daniel, and especially this chapter, is the key to understanding the prophetic Scriptures' (John F. Walvoord, 1971). The prophecy of the Seventy Weeks, as it is usually known, has been called 'the backbone of prophetic chronology'. Many other Scriptures in both Testaments may be correlated by reference to this divine timetable for Israel's history. So, if we do not interpret this Scripture correctly, we shall probably not interpret many other related Scriptures correctly either. In particular, Daniel chapter 9 verses 24-27 are vitally linked with the prophecies found later in the Book of Revelation, since Revelation refers on many occasions to the same timescale as is explained here.

As before, so here we shall interpret the chapter as literally as is reasonable. This will mean that we shall follow the usual Premillennial understanding of it. Other non-literal interpretations only lead to complete confusion. Unbelieving liberal scholars can make very little sense out of the prophecy at the end of the chapter. In fact, it has been called 'the dismal swamp of Old Testament criticism'. The usual Amillennial/ Reformed interpretation, which uses much spiritualisation of references to Israel, applying them to the Church, and attempts to read the New Covenant into the passage, similarly runs into great difficulties in making good sense of it. Only the literal approach yields good sense and results in a clear understanding not only of this passage, but of many other related Scriptures. What is more, history has begun to confirm this literal interpretation in some significant ways concerning the nation of Israel and Jerusalem. Currently, after nearly two thousand years of New Testament history and many hundreds of years of the Jewish Dispersion, they have become the focus of international politics and worldwide anxiety. Premillennial students of Scripture would say that their view of the prophetic Scriptures is being confirmed slowly, but surely, by historical events around us. We do not expect to see the full culmination of the programme for Israel ourselves before the Rapture of the Church, but these events encourage us to lift up our heads in expectancy of the imminent return of the Lord Jesus Himself for us. Maranatha! And soon after we have been translated to heaven, the last part of the prophecy will be fulfilled just as literally as the earlier parts have already been fulfilled.

1. Daniel's Discovery from the Scriptures concerning the End of the Exile, vv.1-2

The events of this chapter occurred just after the Babylonian Empire had been conquered by the Medo-Persian Empire in 539 B.C., during the first year of Darius the Mede's rule over Babylon, so probably during 538 B.C. Daniel was now well over eighty years of age, but still at the height of his mental powers and spiritual character. From his previous visions received during Belshazzar's reign he would not have been surprised by the turn of events in the kingdom. In fact, chapter 6 has told us that the incoming Median king, Darius, immediately conferred high office upon Daniel. The Medo-Persians were somewhat more favourably disposed towards the Jewish people than the previous Babylonian monarchs had been. How far this was due to Daniel's own godly influence upon the affairs of state we cannot be sure; but God was certainly moving behind the scenes to conclude the Babylonian Exile of the Jews.

At all events, Daniel suddenly realised from his reading of the prophet Jeremiah's writings that the Lord had predicted that the Babylonian Exile would last no more than seventy years. He had clearly been reading Jeremiah chapter 25 verses 8-14 and chapter 29 verses 10-14. Since he had been carried away with the first of the three waves of exiled captives in 605 B.C., the starting date for the whole Times of the Gentiles, he must have calculated that the end of the Exile was no more than a few years away. Daniel probably well understood the reason for the exact length of the Captivity. It was in retribution not only for Israel's serious apostasy generally, but in particular for their refusal to observe the sabbatical years as commanded in the Levitical Law (Leviticus chapters 25 and 26), over a period of 490 years since the time of king Solomon. 2 Chronicles chapter 36 verse 21, which must post-date the return from the Exile, also confirms this reason for the seventy year period of discipline for God's people. Truly, the wheels of God's government grind slowly, but they grind exceedingly small! Let us be warned by this fact and fear to grieve our Lord in the first place!

Daniel's reaction to this realisation was most commendable. He did not simply rejoice that soon he and his people could be free and in their own land again. No, because he was very grieved over Israel's sins which had brought such calamity and disgrace both upon the Lord their God and themselves, he decided to pray earnestly for his nation's restoration to their land. It was not something that he just took for granted would happen in a very few years. In this we see the combination of God's sovereignty with the exercise of human responsibility, as everywhere in Scripture; the two are always inseparable, even if inexplicable to us logically. This chapter tells us what began to happen when he did start to pray about his people's sins and their restoration to their land. We shall see that the results of really earnest and heartfelt prayer can sometimes be quite remarkable, and perhaps somewhat unexpected, as was the case here.

2. Daniel's Intercessory Prayer for his people Israel, vv.3-19

Daniel's prayer here is a model of reverence, utter sincerity, and transparent honesty. It should be compared with the other great prayers of confession recorded in Scripture, namely, those of Ezra (recorded in Ezra chapter 9) and Nehemiah and the repentant Jewish remnant (recorded in Nehemiah chapters 1 and 9 respectively). When God sees us thus upon our knees before Him, He will always answer us abundantly above all that we can ask or even think.

His Preparation for Prayer, vv.3-4

When Daniel began to pray, he did not rush irreverently into the Presence of His God. No, he first humbled himself before the Lord by putting on sackcloth and ashes, and exercised self-denial and discipline by fasting. When he did begin to pray, he first of all remembered all that the Lord his God is, worshipping Him for His greatness and faithfulness in true godly fear. After all, the Eternal God already knows all that we intend to say to Him before we start to express it; also He lives in eternity, not time, and so will not be hurried into listening to puny mortals like us. He is always much more concerned that we should become like Him in holy character than in exactly what we have in mind to say to Him. True prayer results in full conformity with His mind and will. Only then can He answer us. Here Daniel was in such a condition of soul and spirit before his God that God answered him by revealing how his people Israel will eventually, after much further severe discipline for their sins against Him, be fully restored to the Lord their covenant God. It is therefore very significant that chapter 9 is the only chapter in the book in which the covenant name of God, Jehovah, the LORD, occurs. And here it is used precisely seven times, the number of divine completeness and perfection, in verses 2, 4, 10, 13, 14 (twice), and 20. How wonderful and appropriate the Word of God is!

His Confession of Sin, vv.5-14
In his confession of Israel's sin Daniel was consciously acting upon the promise contained in Deuteronomy chapter 30 that, if Israel were to repent of their sins, confess them, and return to the Lord their God, they would be delivered from the results of their previous disobedience, namely, captivity by their enemies. For the Lord had predicted the whole of Israel's apostasy and consequent calamities to Moses at the giving of the Law; He foreknew from the beginning the whole sad history, and had prepared a way back for His chosen nation. How gracious and patient He is with His erring people!

Daniel was so humble before the Lord that he confessed his people's sins as if they were his own personally; he fully identified himself with them, as if he had also committed them. Ezra and Nehemiah did exactly the same in their two prayers of confession. This is an example to us today. Are we prepared to do this when things go wrong in our assembly, or in our nation? Or do we take a 'holier than thou' attitude towards our sinning fellow-saints or fellow-nationals, pretending that we are entirely beyond reproach? This is not the mind of Christ, who made Himself fully answerable for all our own sins. Can we not do the same as He? For by nature we are no better than those who have actually committed the sins in question.

Daniel had a great appreciation of the Lord's character; for he spoke of Him as great, awesome, righteous, faithful, merciful, forgiving, true, and holy. And he made no excuses for Israel at all, but spoke with great contrition and humility. The Lord always listens to those who are contrite and broken-hearted about themselves; this is the way to restoration. Daniel accepted that Israel had fully deserved all the disasters that had befallen them, and was mortified that their sins had so disgraced the

Lord's name, which had been set upon His city Jerusalem. He saw clearly the whole history which the Law of Moses had predicted long ago, and he fully justified the Lord in all His acts of judgement against His erring people.

His Petition for Mercy and Restoration, vv.15-19
When Daniel did finally turn to intercede for Israel, he did so not for Israel's sake at all, but in order to protect the Lord's own Name and glory, which were inseparably bound up with Israel's fate. Like Moses before him, Daniel argued that, if Israel were to be finally lost, then the Lord's Name and glory would suffer dishonour and reproach from His enemies, because He had made Israel and the patriarchal fathers many unconditional covenant promises. On that basis alone he pleaded that the Lord would forgive Israel's sins now and restore them to their land again. In this Daniel is a good example of how we should intercede for our erring fellow-believers. We should always consider what outcome will most advance the Lord's glory, rather than our own, or others' blessing.

3. Gabriel's Swift Response, vv.20-23
Verses 20-23 contain the Lord's swift and gracious answer to Daniel's fervent prayer in the form of the angel Gabriel coming to him again, as he had in chapter 8 verse 13, to explain to him more of the Lord's purposes for His people Israel and His city Jerusalem. Daniel had clearly been very confused and upset by the vision given to him in chapter 8, because it spoke of Israel suffering still further for their sins in times well beyond the end of the Babylonian Captivity. The further revelation in verses 24-27 clarified the whole matter for him. Here, as in chapter 10 verses 10 and 19, Gabriel tells Daniel that he is 'a man greatly beloved', or delighted in by his God as a faithful servant. Because 'the secret of the Lord is with them that fear Him', the Lord was revealing to him many of His future purposes for Israel's discipline and ultimate restoration which unbelievers would never be allowed to understand clearly. It is so with us today. God has revealed to us many things which are to come,

because we have come to trust and obey Him, unlike the majority of mankind. How much do we appreciate His love and friendship towards us in this way? But it is also a great responsibility to be in possession of so much understanding of what the future holds for this world in which we live. We should use our prior knowledge both to encourage fellow-saints concerning our ultimate destiny of blessing, and to warn the unsaved of the fate that awaits them, unless they like us repent and believe the gospel.

4. The Revelation of the Prophecy concerning Israel's Further Seventy Weeks of Years, vv.24-27

Verses 24-27 constitute one of the most remarkable and far-reaching panoramic prophecies concerning Israel and Jerusalem in the whole of the Old Testament. Here we have predictions dating from the end of the Babylonian Exile to the Second Coming of Christ in glory. From one point of view it is a very solemn passage, because it shows us just how long the full consequences of serious sin, such as Israel's apostasy from the Lord their God has been, can go on for, and just how much severe discipline is needed to bring His erring people back into normal relationship with Himself again. Although it was true that the Babylonian Captivity of seventy years was nearly over, still beyond that time another seventy times seven years must elapse before the Lord would have finished dealing with His people Israel's sins, another 490 years of His sovereign disciplining hand upon them. The seventy 'sevens' or 'heptads' spoken of here must refer to weeks of years, sets of seven years each, not months or days. No other unit of time makes any sense of the prophecy which follows.

The Summary of God's Ultimate Purposes for Israel, v.24

We should note, first of all, that this prophecy is said to concern Daniel's people, Israel, and Daniel's city, Jerusalem, not the Church. Failure to understand and accept this fact has led many sincere Christians to attempt to see here references to the history of God's present people, the New Testament Church, and to the New Covenant in verse 27. Many Amillennial and Reformed writers have so expounded this passage, but this way of interpreting it leads to complete confusion in understanding both this and other prophetical Scriptures. No, the Church is not mentioned in the Book of Daniel, nor indeed in the Old Testament at all. In Scripture Israel always means the earthly nation of Israel, never the Church; and Jerusalem, or Zion, always means the earthly city of Jerusalem, never heaven.

Verse 24 says that by the time the 490 further years have ended six things will have been completed for God's ancient earthly people Israel. The first three concern Israel's sin and rebellion against Him, while the second three concern the establishment of the millennial kingdom. While it is true to say that the basis for accomplishing the first three things was laid in the sacrificial work of Christ on the cross at His first coming in grace, nevertheless all six will not be fully completed before Christ's Second Coming in glory to reign. God will bring to an end Israel's transgression, or rebellion, against Him only at the Second Coming, when the nation will see the One whom they so wrongly pierced, will repent, turn back to Him, and accept Christ's sacrifice for them. Then, too, He will put an end to their sin, and atone for, or rather purge, their wickedness on the basis of Christ's substitutionary sacrifice as a ransom price paid for them. The second three things mentioned as being accomplished concern the positive aspects of God's future programme for Israel. He will bring in a kingdom of everlasting righteousness when Christ returns to rule for a thousand years and beyond. He will seal up all vision and prophecy, in the sense of bringing to fulfilment all His promises and prophecies, so that there is no longer any further need for visions and prophecies to be given to men. Finally, the reference to the anointing of 'the most holy' probably relates to the anointing , or consecration, of the most holy place, the inner sanctuary, which will be built in the millennial temple, as described in Ezekiel chapters 40-48. The whole prophecy thus extends right up to the Second Coming of Christ in glory and the establishment of Christ's millennial kingdom. It goes far beyond the details and even the immediate effects of Christ's first coming, which Amillennial scholars tend to assert fulfilled the whole prophecy. No, it goes far beyond and past the present Church age to the time of the end.

Predictions concerning the First Sixty-Nine Weeks, v.25
Turning, then, to the detailed predictions of the prophecy, it is first of all important to establish the fact that the 490 years spoken of are prophetic years of 360 days each, rather than the usual solar years of 365 days. That this is the case is proved by comparing the references to the same time period described in three different ways in the Book of Revelation. There what is obviously the same time period is described as either 'time, times, and half a time', that is three and a half years, or as 42 months, or as 1260 days. The equation of 1260 days with 42 months proves that the prophetic month was taken as 30 days. So a prophetic year must be 360 days, and the whole period of the Great Tribulation will last just 1260 days, or 42 months.

Having established that important fact, it is then possible to calculate exactly how long the first 69 weeks of years lasted, namely, 173,880 days. Once we know the starting-point of this period of time, we can then calculate its end to the exact day, or date. Sir Robert Anderson in his book *The Coming Prince*, first published in 1895, demonstrated the results of this calculation. Dr Alva McClain confirmed his general conclusions later in 1940. Their calculations have been questioned a little since then, but remain substantially established as the basis of a literal interpretation of the prophecy.

It is important to take as the starting-point of the fulfilment of the prophecy the commandment issued by Artaxerxes I to rebuild the city of Jerusalem in 445 B.C. in Nehemiah's day (Nehemiah chapter 2 verse 1), not earlier decrees to rebuild the temple issued by Artaxerxes in 458 B.C., nor Cyrus' original decree allowing the Jews to return to their country in 538 B.C. The prophecy speaks clearly about the city and the wall, as in

Nehemiah's day, not the temple or altar, as in Ezra's day and earlier. This provides a basis for calculating the end-date of the 69th week of years, which is said to extend right up to 'Messiah the Prince', who must be Christ Himself. The 69 weeks are divided into two unequal parts, 7 and 62. The first seven weeks of years (49 years of 360 days each) are said to be occupied with the rebuilding of the walls of Jerusalem in troubled times. The Book of Nehemiah bears out this prediction abundantly, although it is unclear what is the end-point historically of the 49 years. Perhaps the end-point was marked by Malachi's day. At all events, Anderson calculated that the next 62 weeks of years ended on 6th April A.D. 32 on the very day when the Lord Jesus rode into Jerusalem on an ass and a colt the foal of an ass, Palm Sunday in our calendar. The Lord's words in Luke chapter 19 verses 41-44 appear to bear this out. He was announcing the fulfilment of the end of this part of the prophecy here on that very day.

Now the exact date and even the year of the crucifixion of Christ are still a matter of some debate. Scholars have argued for various dates between about A.D. 29 and 33. The detailed calculations made by Anderson may not be quite certain, since various astronomical factors have to be taken into account. But the approach is undoubtedly on the right lines, and an answer near to these dates is likely to provide a solution to the problem. A literal interpretation of the prophecy is entirely sound, however exactly it should be worked out.

The Events predicted for the Prophetic Gap in the Sequence, v.26

After the end of the 62 weeks there is clearly in verse 26 a break in the overall sequence of 70 weeks, a 'prophetic gap', in which a few further things are predicted to take place before the last week of years, the 70th, is spoken of in verse 27. During this gap it is predicted that at least two significant events will take place. First, Messiah will be cut off, and have nothing due to Him from Israel. This is a clear prediction of the execution of Christ almost as soon as the 69th week of years had run its course. Christ was judicially 'cut off' by crucifixion. Secondly, 'the people of the prince that shall come shall destroy the city and the sanctuary'. This is a remarkable prediction of the later destruction of Jerusalem and the temple in A.D. 70 by the Romans. But here we are alerted to another 'prince' who is to come from the same Roman people who destroyed the Jewish capital in A.D.70. It is probably he who is referred to in verse 27 in connection with the future 70th week of the prophecy, rather than 'Messiah the Prince' earlier. 'The prince that shall come 'is the nearer antecedent to the 'he' at the beginning of verse 27. Finally, in the latter half of verse 26 the continuing wars over Jerusalem and that whole region ever since then are referred to. History has abundantly confirmed this prediction. It remains to note that the Age of Grace and the New Testament Church fits exactly into this gap in the sequence of the prophecy. It is an axiom of prophetic interpretation that the Church is nowhere the subject of Old Testament prophecy, and that the Age of Grace was not foreseen by the Old Testament prophets, being a 'mystery' hidden in God 'from ages and generations' (see Colossians chapter 1 verse 26 and compare Ephesians chapter 3 verses 4-5) before Christ came to build His Church from the day of Pentecost onwards. Failure to accept that there is a gap in the prophetic programme here has led Amillennial and Reformed interpreters into much confusion and error in understanding this whole prophecy.

Predictions concerning the Seventieth Week, v.27

As we stated in the notes on verse 26, the 'he' of this verse is much more likely to be 'the prince that shall come', a ruler of Roman origin, whatever his nationality, than 'Messiah the Prince' of verse 25. What is said of this future Roman Prince is contrary to Christ's character and purposes; He would never create anything that could be called an abomination nor break His covenant promise, as the person here will do. No, this verse predicts events which will take place during the future Tribulation period, the same period as is referred to in the Book of Revelation and in the Olivet Discourse in Matthew chapter 24 and Mark chapter 13, besides a number of other Old Testament Scriptures, such as Jeremiah chapter 30 verse 7.

This coming evil Roman Prince, therefore, will confirm a covenant with the many, the majority of the Jewish people living in the end times, for one week of years, that is, seven years. This covenant will probably protect them from their enemies and permit them to practise their Jewish religion with sacrifices and temple ritual. It has nothing to do with the New Covenant mentioned in other Scriptures. We know from Matthew chapter 24 and 2 Thessalonians chapter 2 that there will be another temple built in Jerusalem in time to be used during this seven-year period. For three and a half years the Jewish people will use this temple and live in relative security from persecution. But at the mid-point of the week of seven years the Roman Prince, who is probably to be identified with the Man of Sin of 2 Thessalonians chapter 2, the first Beast of Revelation chapter 13, and the Antichrist of 2 John chapter 2, will for some reason break his covenant with Israel, and institute in the temple the worship of an image of himself, claiming that he is God. This image is what is referred to as 'the abomination of desolation' by the Lord Jesus in Matthew chapter 24 verse 15, as well as here. He confirms that this scene is yet future to our day, quoting this reference to it in 'Daniel the prophet'.

The last half of verse 27 is difficult to translate clearly, but the ESV translates as follows: 'And on the wing of abominations shall come one who makes desolate, until the decreed end is poured out on the desolator'. 'The wing of abominations' must be a reference to the idolatrous image of the Beast in the temple, while the 'one who makes desolate' is probably a reference to the Beast himself, who will viciously persecute the Jews and all believers of those times who refuse to bow down to his image and thus worship Satan's man. Revelation chapter 13 reveals the truth about this future persecution, as do Matthew chapter 24 and Mark chapter 13 also. But the length of time during which the Man of Sin will rule, aided by the False Prophet, the second Beast, will be strictly limited to three and a half years. Then, according to Revelation chapter 19, both these evil characters will be destroyed by the Second Coming of Christ, and by the breath of His mouth. This verse does not go into detail concerning the end of 'the prince that shall come', but merely states it emphatically. He will be prevented from completely destroying the whole Jewish nation and all believers when Christ returns in glory to judge and reign.

This, then, is a most remarkable prophecy, from which Old Testament believers could have known to within a few decades when Christ would come the first time in grace. There is no indication in Scripture that anyone did understand this, although a few faithful believers in Luke chapters 1-2 were evidently looking for Him to come. This prophecy will guide future believers who are called to live through the days of the Great Tribulation. They will realise the awful price Israel will be called upon to pay in terms of divine discipline and permitted persecution for their sins of idolatry in Old Testament days and for the crucifixion of their Messiah in New Testament days. Their enemies will be God's instrument in chastising, but not completely destroying, them. We learn here, too, that the first Beast of Revelation chapter 13 will originate from the confines of the Roman Empire, even though he may prove to be an apostate Jew like the second Beast. Finally, we learn that the signing of a false peace treaty by the Beast with Israel will be the signal for the start of the whole Tribulation period of seven years. We just do not know how long after the Rapture of the Church this signing may take place. Today we see the world shaping up for the fulfilment of these end time events, and therefore look up in eager expectation of our own Rapture to heaven, which must take place before all this can begin to unfold. Maranatha!

CHAPTER 10

Daniel's Final Vision of the Lord and the Revelation of Angelic Warfare

The last three chapters of the book record a remarkable prediction of future events that is almost without parallel in Scripture for its minute detail, especially in chapter 11. So much so, that many commentators even amongst believers have doubted that it was written before the events took place. But simple faith in an Almighty, sovereign, and omniscient God does believe this, particularly since some of the events predicted are clearly still future to our own day.

Chapter 10 forms an extensive introduction to this long passage of predictive prophecy; in fact, chapter 11 verse 1 completes this introduction. The next section, chapter 11 verse 2 to 12 verse 4, divides into two major divisions. First, chapter 11 verses 2-35 deal with the immediate future, from Darius the Mede to Antiochus Epiphanes; while, secondly, chapter 11 verse 36 to 12 verse 4 deals with the far future, the events of the end times just before the Second Coming of Christ. Chapter 12 verses 5-13 contain a final message and revelation to Daniel.

Daniel's fourth vision gathers together the various significant threads of prophecy relating to Israel and their history under Gentile dominion.

1. The Date and Nature of the Vision, v.1
Daniel received this vision in the third year of Cyrus king of Persia, therefore in 536 B.C. He probably lived at least a few

more years beyond this date to write this book in which the vision is recorded. There is no conflict here with the statement in chapter 1 verse 21 that 'Daniel continued even unto the first year of king Cyrus', since that statement does not necessarily mean that he died then, but that he survived all the events of the Babylonian Empire triumphantly and saw at least the beginning of the Medo-Persian Empire. The reference to his Babylonian name, Belteshazzar, serves to confirm that he was the same person as was known by that name under Nebuchadnezzar's rule earlier in the book. The 'thing' that was revealed to Daniel would be better translated 'a word'. This word was true, and involved a 'great warfare', a 'great task', or a 'great conflict', probably with the idea of 'involved great suffering'. The Hebrew expression used here is difficult to translate, but probably implies that the period in view in the vision is a long and difficult one, and involves great conflict and suffering for Israel, the people of God. By contrast with the previous visions, Daniel is said to have understood this final vision.

2. Daniel's Preparation to receive the Vision, vv.2-3

Daniel was so troubled concerning his people and their fate that he spent three full weeks mourning, only eating the basic necessities of life. Probably he had heard of the difficulties being faced by the returned Jewish exiles in Jerusalem and district. He probably felt responsible for having encouraged their return into such a situation. He himself was now clearly too old to attempt to join the returned remnant, and could do more for them by staying in Babylon and praying for them. Note that the three weeks here are explicitly said to be 'of days', not years, unlike the seventy weeks of years in the previous chapter.

3. Daniel's Vision of the Glory of the Lord, vv.4-9

We are not told how long it was after the three weeks had elapsed that Daniel had this vision, but it was on the twenty-fourth day of the first month, which was known as Abib or later as Nisan, and occurred while he was standing beside the river Hiddekel, or Tigris. This proves that Daniel had not returned to Jerusalem with the small Jewish remnant. In this place he saw a vision of a glorious man clothed in linen and girded with fine gold of Uphaz. His body was like a beryl, his face like lightning, while his eyes resembled lamps of fire. His arms and feet looked like coloured brass, and his voice sounded like that of a great crowd. Bible students have debated the identity of this 'heavenly man', but it seems most likely that this was a Theophany, an appearance of the pre-incarnate Son of God in human form. He seems to be much more glorious than all the angels mentioned later in the chapter, and some aspects of the description of his appearance resemble quite closely those of the risen glorified Christ in Revelation chapter 1, particularly his eyes, feet, face, and voice. And the vision had a similar effect on Daniel to the effect John's vision of Christ had upon him. He was completely overcome by it, so that he had no strength left in him. The people who were with him did not see the vision, but were visibly shaken by the event and fled to hide themselves from the presence of the Lord. But Daniel did hear the voice of the Lord who had appeared to him. It had the effect of sending him into a deep sleep. In this condition of utter weakness he received further revelation from angelic beings.

4. An Angel revives Daniel and reveals to him Angelic Conflicts, vv.10-14

All the angels mentioned in the remainder of the chapter seem to be distinct from the 'heavenly man' of verses 4-6; none have His glory or almighty power such as is associated with Deity alone. Here an angel revives Daniel and raises him on to his hands and knees. Then he reassures the trembling old saint that he was a man greatly beloved, which meant that God was going to reveal to him His purposes for His people Israel over a very long period right up to the end times. In fact, God had sent this angel on a special mission to Daniel to do this. Some believers live so close to the Lord that He treats them as the objects of His special love and favour, and shows them things that He shares with no-one else. Are we each one 'dwelling in the secret place of the Most High'? Or, most relevantly to us today, are we 'abiding in Christ' in closest fellowship with Him daily?

Now the angel reveals to Daniel that his earnest prayer for his people Israel in verses 1-2 had not been ignored at all, but only delayed in being answered by a great unseen angelic conflict being waged in the international affairs of the major kingdoms of the time. An evil angelic prince of Persia had resisted this holy angel from God in his mission to Daniel during the whole three weeks of his prayer. In fact, it had been necessary for the archangel Michael, the angel with special responsibility for Israel, to come to assist the other angel against this evil angelic prince. Even the holy angels are not omnipotent like their God.

How instructive this passage of Scripture is for all believers today as well as for Daniel. First of all, concerning our prayers; for it assures us that there is always a good reason why they are not necessarily answered immediately, even when we are asking according to the mind and will of God. Secondly, concerning the spiritual and heavenly warfare in which every believer is inevitably involved in our own day as well as in Daniel's day, it tells us that there is much going on in heavenly places that we know nothing directly about, a great conflict between the forces of God and good and the forces of Satan and evil. Ephesians chapter 6 tells us about this also, and prescribes necessary spiritual armour for the Christian today to put on, if he is to stand against his spiritual foes and win the battle with Satan. But ultimately victory is assured to the trusting saint today, as in Daniel's day. Calvary's cross and Christ's resurrection have accomplished that!

5. Daniel is strengthened again by Angels, vv.15-19
Again, Daniel was overwhelmed by his supernatural experiences, and became dumb. But a person resembling a man, probably an angel not a Theophany here, touched his lips, so

that he was able to express his thoughts again. He said that the vision had troubled him and also completely exhausted him. He did not know how he could continue to listen to the angel. Then another angel, possibly different from the previous one, touched Daniel again and reassured him that he was a man greatly beloved of his God, so that he really had no cause for fear. He blessed him with God's peace and told him to be strong. At this Daniel was strengthened for the third time to listen further to the vision to be revealed to him. The detail given to Daniel's experiences here suggests that the revelation which follows in chapters 11 and 12 is of tremendous significance and importance, as indeed we shall find to be the case. Daniel's agonising experience here is very similar to that of our Lord in the Garden of Gethsemane, where He too received the strengthening ministry of angels. We do not realise how much we today owe to the ministry of angels.

6. The Revelation of further Angelic Conflict and the Introduction to the Long Vision, vv.20-21

The stage has thus been set for the great revelation that follows. The angel asks Daniel if he knows why he has been sent to him, and proceeds to explain that he must now leave him to return to fight with the evil angelic prince of Persia, who had undoubtedly been trying to frustrate God's purposes of restoration for His people Israel. After that he would need to confront the angelic prince of Greece. We thus learn that behind the many details of prophecy relating to human history there is an unseen struggle between good and evil angelic forces that God's will may be done. The angel now says that he will reveal to Daniel what is recorded in heaven in a book called 'the scripture of truth'. The facts which are now to be revealed are already in God's record in heaven, and are to become part of the Holy Scriptures on earth. This indicates that the eternal plan of God is even greater than that part of it which is contained in the Bible. 'The scripture of truth' reflects God's full sovereign will to be accomplished in the world. So Daniel was assured of the certainty of the things which he was about to be told.

Finally, concerning the spiritual struggle which the vision will unfold, the angel says that he and Michael, the Archangel prince, are the only angels responsible for the welfare of Daniel's people Israel. Michael is mentioned in this chapter for the first time in Scripture. Other references to him are found in chapter 12 verse 1, Jude verse 9, and Revelation chapter 12.

It has been observed that the fact that a whole chapter is devoted to the preparation for the vision that follows indicates just how important that vision is for God's purposes in the world.

CHAPTER 11

The Vision continued with the Prediction of the Wars of the Kings of the North and South

1. *The Conclusion of the Introduction to the Vision, v.1*

Verse 1 really belongs to chapter 10, since in it the angel concludes his introduction to the vision which follows. Having stated at the end of chapter 10 that only he and the archangel Michael, the prince of the Jewish people, were available to withstand the evil angels who opposed them and sought their downfall, he continues by saying that at the beginning of the reign of Darius the Mede, which marked the transition from the Babylonian Empire to the Medo-Persian Empire, he had stood up to strengthen him. Now the 'him' here could refer either to Michael or to Darius the Mede. Possibly, it is better to understand the reference to be to Michael, in view of the end of chapter 10, but the other view is also tenable. Certainly, Darius the Mede showed remarkable favour towards Daniel as soon as he came to the throne of Babylon.

2. *The Predicted History of later Persian and Greek Kings, vv.2-4*

The same angel now announces that he is going to show Daniel the truth about the future of his people under Gentile dominion. All that is predicted here up to verse 35 has already been fulfilled so accurately that some Bible commentators have thought it to be recorded history rather than pure prediction; but our God is able in His sovereign eternity both to foresee and to control all events, so that we need not be surprised by these remarkable prophecies. This assures us that the remainder of the chapter from verse 36 to verse 45 will also be fulfilled in its right time in a similar exact and literal way; for the events predicted in these latter verses have never yet happened.

Verse 2 predicts that four more kings will arise in the Persian Empire, of whom the fourth will be by far the strongest and richest. This was fulfilled in the reigns of Cambyses (529-522 B.C.), who is not mentioned in the Old Testament, Pseudo-Smerdis (522-521 B.C.), who reigned only briefly, Darius I Hystaspes (521-486 B.C.), who is mentioned in Ezra chapters 5 and 6, and Xerxes I (486-465 B.C.), who is probably to be identified with Ahasuerus of Esther and Ezra chapter 4 verse 6. Now Darius I had invaded Greece in 490 B.C., but had been defeated by the Greeks at the Battle of Marathon. This explains why Xerxes, who was by far the richest emperor of Persia, also invaded Greece in 481-479 B.C. with a huge army of two and a half million men to avenge the earlier defeat. But he in his turn was decisively defeated by the Greeks in a famous naval battle in the Bay of Salamis in 480 B.C. and again on land at Plataea and Mycale in 479 B.C. Xerxes retreated in humiliation, and the Persian Empire was never so strong again after this. That is probably the reason why none of the later kings of Persia are mentioned here, and the prophecy continues with the much later reign of Alexander the Great, the mightiest king of Greece there has ever been, who accomplished so much in the brief period between 336 and 323 B.C. He conquered the whole Persian Empire in a few years, but then suddenly died at almost 33 years of age, leaving his vast empire to be divided between his four strongest generals, since none of his sons survived him very long. The reference here to 'the four winds of heaven' clearly refers to these generals, who have been named earlier in the commentary. Much of the subsequent chapter concerns the wars between two of them, the Ptolemies of Egypt, the so-called 'king of the south', and the Seleucids of Syria/Palestine, the so-called 'king of the north', south and north, that is, of the land of Israel.

3. The Predicted Wars between the Ptolemies and the Seleucids across the Promised Land, vv.5-20

This complicated and tedious prediction of the continual conflicts between the Ptolemies in the south and the Seleucids in the north may seem rather barren in terms of spiritual significance for us today. But the very fact that it was all predicted to Daniel in the sixth century B.C., long before it all occurred, is remarkable evidence of God's sovereign control of all history, especially as it relates to His people Israel and their land; for these wars were conducted all across Israel's Promised Land. This passage of Scripture, therefore, is clear proof of the divine inspiration of all Scripture. Only the almighty God of Israel could have foretold all this in such accurate detail as we find here; for all the historical events predicted, albeit often in a slightly symbolical way, have been verified by Biblical historians in the past two hundred years. This is a cause of unbelief in liberal theologians, but of grateful acceptance by true Christians. It confirms the latter's faith, but leads unbelievers to invent other improbable explanations for the facts here recorded.

What, then, is the meaning of the prophecies which follow in verses 5-20, which are now to us simply ancient history? We shall attempt to summarize this under the reigns of the various opposing kings, who together span about one hundred and fifty years, from 323-175 B.C.

Verse 5: Ptolemy I Soter (323-285 B.C.) and Seleucus I Nicator (312-281 B.C.)

First, therefore, Seleucus had fled from Antigonus of Babylon and allied himself with Ptolemy I of Egypt to defeat Antigonus and rule from Asia Minor to India. Thus he became stronger than Ptolemy, as this verse predicts that he would.

Verse 6: The Alliance between Ptolemy II Philadelpus (285-246 B.C.) and Antiochus II Theos (261-246 B.C.)

After some years, which is the meaning of AV 'in the end of

years', the king of the south, Egypt, a Ptolemy, wished to make an alliance with the current king of the north, Antiochus II, by the marriage of his daughter, Berenice, to the latter. In order to do this, Antiochus was required to divorce his true wife, Laodice. But Berenice was unable to achieve the purpose of this political marriage, the meaning of the phrase 'she shall not retain the strength of her arm', because within two years Ptolemy II died, Antiochus took back his wife Laodice, and then the rejected Laodice took her revenge on all of them by murdering her husband, Antiochus, his Egyptian wife Berenice, and their infant son. What a sad story of intrigue, treachery, and revenge! But such is the human heart.

Verses 7-9: Ptolemy III Euergetes (246-241 B.C.) and Seleucus Callinicus (247-226 B.C.)

Now, however, Berenice's brother, Ptolemy III Euergetes, took his late father's place, and attacked the then-current king of the north, Seleucus Callinicus, overcame him, and carried off much treasure and some princes as hostages back to Egypt. The end of verse 8 means that he would refrain from attacking the king of the north for some years. Verse 9 in the AV is also a mistranslation. It really means that the king of the north will come into the realm of the king of the south, but be repulsed and return to his own land, Syria, again. So began a seesaw battle between Egypt and Syria. But probably the point of explaining this conflict so far was to prepare the way for the main subject of verses 10-19, which is the later ascendancy of Syria, the king of the north, over Egypt, the king of the south, and the return of the Promised Land to the control of the kings of the north; for the angel was going to predict that under the most notorious of the latter kings, Antiochus Epiphanes, Israel would be severely persecuted, according to verses 21-35.

Verses 10-19: The Conflict between Seleucus Ceraunus and Antiochus the Great of Syria and Ptolemy Philopator of Egypt, 226-187 B.C.

The predicted history becomes quite complicated at this point, but it has all been fulfilled to the smallest detail. God was in complete control of all these kings' movements over His people's land. The Syrian sons, or rather successors, of Seleucus Callinicus were more successful than he in their attack on Egypt. But one of them, Seleucus Ceraunus III (226-223 B.C.), died in battle in Asia Minor, leaving the other, Antiochus III the Great (223-187 B.C.), to continue the struggle. In anger that the Syrians had encroached so far upon Egyptian territory, Ptolemy Philopator (221-203 B.C.) assembled a large army to confront Antiochus in battle at Raphia on the border of Palestine in 217 B.C. The Egyptians gained a complete victory on that occasion, despite the size of Antiochus's army; 'the multitude' of the latter's army was 'given into his (Ptolemy's) hand', as predicted here. However, Ptolemy Philopator did not follow up his victory effectively, but squandered all his advantages over his enemy in licentious living, indolence, and proud self-confidence. He and his queen died in mysterious circumstances in 203 B.C. Pride comes before destruction, and a haughty spirit before a fall!

Consequently, in 201 B.C. Antiochus III, who had been preoccupied for some years with conquests in the east of his realm, was able to reassemble another large army and attack Egypt again, this time more successfully than before, as predicted in verses 13-16. The reference in verse 14 to 'the robbers of thy people' is to a large number of Jews who entered into a league with Antiochus III against Egypt, and joined in his attacks upon that land. The Egyptians had actually treated the Jews quite favourably, so the prophecy views their treachery with disapproval. The many who would stand up at that time against the king of the south included Philip of Macedon, rebels within Egypt itself, and these 'violent men' amongst Daniel's own people, the Jews. The general revolt against Ptolemy would unwittingly help to fulfil God's purpose in chastening His people under Antiochus Epiphanes, as already outlined in chapter 8. This rebellion would thus result in the fulfilment of the vision given earlier to Daniel. However, the rebels failed in their own real object of making Judaea independent; in this way 'they stumbled so as to fall'.

Verse 15 predicts the defeat of the Egyptian general Scopas by Antiochus III at Paneas, and the former's surrender at Sidon, which is the 'well-fortified city' referred to here, despite reinforcements sent to help him. Verse 16 means that nothing will prevent the king of the north taking full control of 'the glorious land', that is, Israel, and that he will be able to destroy it. Verse 17 then predicts that Antiochus will determine to regain the full control that his predecessor Seleucus I Nicator of verse 5 had enjoyed over these lands. The enigmatic reference to 'upright ones with him' may be a derogatory and ironical one against those of the Jews who had sided with him. The word is 'Jeshurun', an ancient description of Israel as 'upright'. In reality, the Jewish rebels were anything but 'upright'. At all events, Antiochus would determine to destroy Egypt without openly attacking it, since he feared intervention by Rome if he did so. So he would arrange to give the young Ptolemy V Epiphanes his daughter Cleopatra as his wife, intending to corrupt him by this means. But the scheme would backfire on him; for Cleopatra would decide to take her new husband's side, not her father's, and even encourage an alliance between Egypt and Rome. Seeing that he would not be able to gain a great empire by this means, Antiochus would direct his attention towards the coastlands of Asia Minor and capture many of them. Then a 'prince', a magistrate or commander, actually the Roman consul Lucius Scipio Asiaticus in the fulfilment, would put an end to his 'reproach', or rather insolence, and turn it back upon Antiochus. This is a reference to Antiochus' scornful treatment of the Roman ambassadors at a conference held at Lysimachia to warn him not to interfere in Greece. In the fulfilment Antiochus ignored the warning, attacked Greece in 192 B.C, but was defeated in 191 B.C. at Thermopylae and again in 189 B.C. at Magnesia, and had to accept humiliating peace terms from the Romans. So Antiochus III the Great, who would have been one of the great conquerors of the ancient world if he had left Greece alone, fulfilled the prophecies of verse 19, that he would return to his own land defeated and broken. There he would 'stumble and fall', assassinated at Elymais in 187 B.C. while raiding the treasures of one of his own temples, and would thus disappear from the page of history. As an accurate description of the history of this period this prophecy bears the unmistakable stamp of divine inspiration. There is no other reasonable explanation for it.

<u>Verse 20: Seleucus IV Philopator, the Raiser of Taxes (187-175 B.C.)</u>
Antiochus the Great was succeeded by Seleucus III Philopator, who oppressed the people of Israel by his heavy taxation. He did this because the Romans had forced him to pay tribute to them, and he acquired the necessary money from his subject peoples, including the Jews. A tax collector called Heliodorus, who is referred to in 2 Maccabees chapter 3 verse 7, took treasures from the temple at Jerusalem to obtain the money from the Jews. But soon after Heliodorus did this, Seleucus Philopator was suddenly and mysteriously removed, 'neither in anger, nor in battle', but possibly by poison given to him by Heliodorus himself. All this would thus set the scene for the advent of the greatest persecutor of the Jews in ancient times, Antiochus IV Epiphanes (175-164 B.C.).

4. The Predicted Campaigns of Antiochus IV Epiphanes and his Persecution of the Jews, vv.21-35

Antiochus Epiphanes is given prominence in this chapter because he persecuted the Jews, Daniel's people, and in this way foreshadowed the arch-persecutor of Israel, the Man of Sin, the first Beast of Revelation chapter 13, the Antichrist of the end times, who is the subject of the remainder of the chapter in verses 36-45, there called the 'wilful king'. Antiochus Epiphanes has already been introduced to us in chapter 8 as the 'little horn' from the Grecian kingdom of Syria who opposed the people of God. Now his reign is described again in somewhat fuller detail. Readers should be aware that many of these predicted historical details were later recorded in the Apocryphal, but largely true, Books of the Maccabees.

Verses 21-23: His Accession and Early Reign

Antiochus Epiphanes was not the natural successor to the throne of Syria, but he obtained it by treachery and flattery. He is described as a 'vile', or despicable, person. A younger son of Seleucus IV Philopator, another Antiochus, was the natural heir, but was murdered by Heliodorus, who hoped to succeed him, and meanwhile another son of the late Seleucus, Demetrius, was being held hostage in Rome at the same time. Antiochus Epiphanes as the brother of Seleucus would take advantage of the situation to seize power by flattery and intrigue in an otherwise bloodless coup. Verse 22 refers to his complete defeat of the armies of Egypt, who were in league with Heliodorus. The latter attempted to deprive Antiochus of power soon after his accession, but failed and disappeared. Compare chapter 9 verse 26 for the same meaning of a 'flood' as a military onslaught. The battle took place in 170 B.C. at a place now called Ras Baron. The reference to the breaking of 'the prince of the covenant' is to the murder by Antiochus of the Jewish high priest, Onias III, in 172 B.C., which heralded many further troubles for the Jews during Antiochus' reign. Then there is a prediction of a 'league made with him'. This refers to an alliance made by Antiochus with Ptolemy VI Philometor of Egypt against Ptolemy VII Euergetes II, his rival for the Egyptian throne. By this means Antiochus deceitfully planned to gain greater power in Egypt, and for a time succeeded in this objective.

Verses 24-26: Antiochus at the Height of his Power

Using every underhanded means available to him Antiochus would set about obtaining complete control of Egypt. In this he succeeded for some years, but the prophecy states that it would be only for a set time, that is, God's time permitted to him; for He is always sovereign over man's plans for empire. Antiochus waged a few campaigns against the Egyptians during these years, and the Egyptian king, 'the king of the south', could not withstand his military power. Antiochus defeated Ptolemy VI Philometor in 169 B.C.

Verses 27-28: Antiochus is Frustrated and Turns against the Jewish People instead

However, the tide would now begin to turn against Antiochus. The victorious Antiochus and his defeated nephew, Ptolemy Philometor, would hold a conference at which both of them would tell many lies about their intentions. Antiochus would pretend to help Ptolemy Philometor regain the throne of Egypt from his brother, Ptolemy Euergetes. But in the event the two Egyptian brothers agreed to rule jointly, thus frustrating Antiochus' scheme to gain control of Egypt in their place. The last part of verse 27 indicates that, in spite of all his intrigues, Antiochus would not succeed. Instead, God's predetermined end for Egyptian rule would only come in His own time and way. Frustrated in Egypt, Antiochus would plunder that land and then return to Syria. Also, he would hear reports of rebellion in Jerusalem, occasioned by his murder of Onias III. So, instead of pursuing his Egyptian designs further he would turn his frustrated wrath against the Jewish people and state, here called the 'holy covenant', and persecute them.

Verses 29-31: Opposed by Rome Antiochus Persecutes the Jews

The first words of verse 29 indicate that the whole plan of Antiochus' life would be predetermined by God, no matter what the evil king's own intentions might be. Certainly, in the historical fulfilment he never enjoyed such success as he had had up until this time. Two further invasions of Egypt were largely unsuccessful, the second because he was met in 168 B.C. near Alexandria by a naval fleet under the Roman consul, Gaius Popillius Laenas, who demanded that he leave Egypt forthwith. This was the fulfilment of the prophecy concerning the 'ships of Chittim', or Kittim in some translations, the Kittim being the Romans, coming, as they did, from the direction of Cyprus. In fact, the Septuagint here translates the whole phrase 'the ships of Chittim' by the name 'the Romans'. The armies of the coming fourth world empire, Rome, were thus beginning to impact upon the weakening power of the third, the Greek, empire.

Antiochus' reaction was alarming. Instead of quietly accepting defeat, he decided to give vent to his wrath upon the comparatively weak Jewish people, who were in a holy covenant with God. The Books of Maccabees record how he gained the allegiance of some Jewish apostates in his persecution of the rest of the Jewish people, whom he murdered in large numbers as he marched through Judaea. Antiochus consummated his atrocities by desecrating the altar in the Jewish temple, offering a sow upon it, forbidding the continuation of the daily sacrifices, and setting up an idol, probably an image of Zeus, in the holy place. The latter idolatrous image would be 'the abomination that maketh desolate' referred to in verse 31. It clearly prefigures and foreshadows the 'abomination of desolation' which the Man of Sin, the first Beast of Revelation chapter 13, will one day set up in the rebuilt temple in Jerusalem at the mid-point of the Tribulation. Daniel refers to this idol in chapters 9 verse 27 and 12 verse 11, as does the Lord Jesus in His Olivet discourse in Matthew 24 verse 15. It will be the signal for the onset of the greatest period of persecution the world will ever know. All that Antiochus did will be repeated by the Man of Sin when he attempts to assume divine powers for himself and demands universal worship.

Verses 32-35: the Revolt of the Maccabees and the Sufferings of the Faithful Jews

The result of this act of sacrilege amongst the Jewish people was two-fold. Some were persuaded by Antiochus' flattery to become traitors to their own nation, and so were corrupted by him. But many others, in particular the family of Judas Maccabeus and his supporters, decided with the help of the Romans to lead a revolt against the oppressing rule of Antiochus. They are described as people who 'know their God', are 'strong', and 'do exploits' of great heroism against huge odds. Those who are described as 'they that understand among the people' would 'instruct many', perhaps from these very chapters of Daniel's prophecy, which had predicted the whole story. The cost to the freedom-fighters in the tiny Jewish state would be great in terms of suffering and martyrdom for some considerable time, and they would receive little help, while the traitors would support Antiochus against them. Even some of those who understood the truth of the Scriptures would suffer also. But God would have a gracious purpose in allowing their suffering; it would refine them of all spiritual dross and prepare them for their ultimate reward in eternity.

At the end of the passage predicting the career and persecutions of Antiochus against the Jews there is a reference to 'the time of the end' and 'a time appointed'. This verse thus prepares us for the transition in the prophecy from the reign of Antiochus Epiphanes to that of the 'wilful king' in the remaining section of the chapter. The latter character clearly belongs to the distant future from Daniel's day, and the details of his reign have never yet been fulfilled. By contrast, the first 35 verses of chapter 11 have all received a very exact and full fulfilment, thus confirming the divine inspiration of Scripture and Daniel's genuineness as a prophet of the Lord.

5. *The Description of the Wilful King of the End Times, vv.36-39*
Antiochus Epiphanes clearly typified this last ruler of the times of Gentile dominion over Israel, Daniel's beloved people. That is why so much space has been given to the prediction of Antiochus' reign. History will repeat itself over many generations; for the heart of man remains the same, absolutely opposed to God and wanting to put himself in the place of God. Both Antiochus and the 'wilful king' here will attempt to do just this, as other Scriptures also confirm.

Now amongst conservative, believing, Premillennial Bible students there are two different views as to who this 'wilful king' will be. Firstly, there are those who identify him with the second Beast of Revelation chapter 13, link him also with the Man of Sin of 2 Thessalonians chapter 2 and the Antichrist of 1 John chapter 2, and hold that he will be an apostate Jew. Some also identify him with the 'king of fierce countenance' of Daniel chapter 8 and the 'idol shepherd' of Zechariah chapter 11. Secondly, there are many others who identify him with the first Beast of Revelation chapter 13, the Roman Prince of Daniel chapter 9, the little horn of Daniel chapter 7, the 'king of fierce countenance' of Daniel chapter 8, the 'idol shepherd' of Zechariah chapter 11, the Man of Sin of 2 Thessalonians chapter 2, and the Antichrist of 1 John chapter 2, and hold that he will be an ungodly Gentile. Since the wilful king described here is clearly the chief ruler in the world of those days, subordinate to no other, it is perhaps difficult to identify him with the second Beast of Revelation chapter 13, because the latter is definitely subordinate to the first Beast there, his henchman as the False Prophet. Many would hold that Revelation chapter 13 is the only reference in Scripture to the second Beast, whereas others think that some of the other Scriptures cited above also refer to him. Perhaps the matter is not completely clear and we should respect those who differ from us on this difficult question.

The main reasons why Bible students have thought that this king must be an apostate Jew from the land of Israel are: first, that the Jews would hardly accept as their Messiah a Gentile such as the first Beast appears to be; and, secondly, that this 'wilful king' is said not to 'regard the God of his fathers', which is taken to refer to the God of Israel. But the phrase 'the God of his fathers' can quite justifiably be translated 'the gods of his fathers', since *Elohim* can refer either to the One true God in the plural form of His name, or to the pagan gods of the Gentile nations around them. So the matter is unclear on the basis of this verse alone. Perhaps the 'wilful king' will disregard gods of any kind, including that of his own people, if he is an apostate Jew. But just as Antiochus Epiphanes who prefigured him was a Gentile, so it would seem possible that the 'wilful king' will also be a Gentile. However, his acceptability to the Jewish people as such remains a serious problem. The matter is somewhat difficult to resolve from the various relevant Scriptures, and may only become clear when the fulfilment takes place.

These verses contain other features of the character of this evil person who will gain such power over his own people. First, he will be completely self-willed, exalt himself, and magnify himself above every god, including the One true God, whose worship he will seek to replace with that of himself. In fact he will speak blasphemously against the true God, claiming to be God himself. In all these respects he is to be identified with the first Beast of Revelation chapter 13, rather than the second Beast, who will merely promote the ambitions of the first Beast. He will succeed in his objectives for a limited time, 'until the indignation be accomplished', which probably refers to the divine judgements of the Great Tribulation upon him and his kingdom. The angel explains to Daniel that what God has determined to do to him will be accomplished in His own time and way. His reign of rebellion and terror will be brought to an abrupt end when God intervenes to check him in his mad career.

Secondly, we have already discussed the phrase 'neither shall he regard the God (or gods) of his fathers'; he will be completely ungodly and defiant of all gods, true or false. Thirdly, he will not regard 'the desire of women'. This could be understood in any of three ways. It may mean that he will be celibate by choice; or it may mean that he will be a homosexual; or, perhaps more probably, it may mean that he will have no regard for Christ, whose mother every godly Jewish woman desired to be. In any case, he will be totally warped spiritually. Instead of honouring any god at all, he will honour 'the God of forces', which probably means that he will rely upon military might alone, not any spiritual faith. 'A god whom his fathers knew not' in verse 38, also described as 'a strange god' in verse 39, may be a prediction of his worship of Satan or his own claim to deity and demand that all men worship him as if he were God, as is predicted clearly in Revelation chapter 13 of the first Beast. He will accumulate great treasures of material things and precious metals and stones for his master, Satan, and himself, and the last part of the verse may mean that he will favour those who follow him by giving them a place in his administration. It must be said that all this more naturally describes the first Beast of Revelation chapter 13 than the second Beast, his subordinate lieutenant in crime.

6. The Campaign of Armageddon and the Fate of the Wilful King, vv.40-45

This passage clearly predicts the war in which the 'wilful king' will become embroiled 'at the time of the end', that is, during the second half of the Great Tribulation period. The timing of it may well be inferred from the prediction in Revelation chapter 16 of the events of the sixth bowl judgement, when the River Euphrates is dried up to make way for the invasion of the Middle East by the armies of the 'kings of the East', and three demonic spirits, using counterfeit miracles, will persuade the other nations of the world to invade the Middle East. The result described there is the campaign of Armageddon, which will take place just prior to the close of the Great Tribulation. This perfectly aligns with the predictions here in Daniel chapter 11 of the final world war which centres on the 'wilful king'. So it probably refers to the same campaign; and we can be fairly certain that the 'time of the end' here means the closing stages of the second half of Daniel's seventieth week of years described in chapter 9. It probably, therefore, does not refer to the beginning of the second half of that week of years. The passage ends with the destruction of the 'wilful king' by God supernaturally. This fully accords with the prediction in Revelation chapter 19 of the fate of the two Beasts in the lake of fire after their capture at Armageddon.

It should be stated that the most natural way of understanding the passage is to interpret the occurrences of 'he' and 'him' throughout it as referring to the 'wilful king', rather than to anyone else, such as the king of the north, who is introduced into the war scene in verse 40. Some expositors have thought that the 'he' in the middle of verse 40 and subsequently will be the king of the north, not the wilful king. This alters the meaning of the passage considerably, as we shall indicate, but is a much less likely interpretation of it. No, the passage predicts the outbreak of a world war against the supreme authority and control of the 'wilful king', the first Beast of Revelation chapter 13. The king of the south, probably Egypt and her pan-African allies, and the king of the north, a pan-Middle Eastern and northern confederacy of nations, will rebel against him and mount an all-out attack against him in Israel. Very probably both of them will be Muslim by religion then, as they are even today, and resent the Beast's claim to deity. The king of the north will come against the 'wilful king' with a large army and navy, but the latter will defeat the forces of the king of the north and move victoriously into many other countries to take spoils of war from them. Edom, Moab, and Ammon will escape his advance, perhaps because the persecuted Jewish remnant will be divinely protected there at that time, according to Revelation chapter 12, and perhaps also because God intends to judge those particular nations Himself in the person of Christ when He returns through His people Israel, as Isaiah chapter 63 and a few other prophecies seem to indicate. The Beast will include Egypt in his conquests and be poised to engulf Libya and Ethiopia also with all their wealth, when disturbing news out of the east and north reaches him and causes him to turn back to the Middle East again to complete his victorious campaign. Clearly, the news from the east will be that of the invasion by the kings of the east, such as China and India with their allies, as Revelation chapter 16 predicts. The news from the north could refer to a Russian invasion. The latter will probably be one later than that predicted in Ezekiel chapters 38 and 39, because that particular invasion will be mounted when Israel is dwelling safely in 'un-walled villages' (Ezekiel 38.11), that is, without military defences to protect them. This situation will only pertain during the first half of the Tribulation, before the

Beast breaks his seven-year covenant with Israel to defend them. Russia and her allies, who are most likely to be identified with Gog and Magog of Ezekiel's prophecy, will probably attack Israel during this first half of the Tribulation and be defeated by God's direct and supernatural intervention in judgement against them. But later on they could possibly regroup and attack again. However that may be, the Beast will set up his headquarters in the middle of Israel, 'the glorious holy mountain', intending to repulse all-comers. There he will come to his end, as we know from Revelation chapter 19, by God's direct action in judgement at the Second Coming of Christ in glory to reign, banished summarily to the lake of fire. Thus his reign of terror and his ambition to be worshipped as God will be brought to an end.

We mentioned earlier another view involving the king of the north, which was that it would be he who would overcome the 'wilful king' and invade many other countries, rather than the 'wilful king', and that it would be the king of the north who would come to his end in Israel at God's hand. Some even hold that the king of the north is to be identified with the Antichrist. Others think that it will be the king of the north who will inflict the 'deadly wound' on the 'wilful king', the first Beast, as predicted in Revelation chapter 13, from which he will recover by Satanic power in a pseudo-resurrection. But there are a few objections to that interpretation of the passage. First of all, it would divide the passage here between two evil men rather than just one, first the 'wilful king' in verse 40a, but then secondly the king of the north in verses 40b to 45. This is unlikely, because the subject throughout the previous chapter has led up to the introduction of the 'wilful king' here, rather than to just another king of the north. The 'wilful king', not so much the king of the north, is the antitype of Antiochus Epiphanes, the previous great persecutor of the Jews. This passage is best understood to refer to the 'wilful king' throughout. Secondly, the Beast of Revelation chapter 13 will receive his 'deadly wound' at the mid-point of the Tribulation, not towards its end, which must be the time here in Daniel chapter 11, because it is his pseudo-resurrection which convinces the world that he must be divine and leads on to his setting up of his image in the rebuilt temple and demanding universal worship. No, this view, interesting though it is, does not explain either this passage or other related passages of Scripture so well as the one advocated above, namely, that it refers to the 'wilful king' throughout.

So ends this long and complicated chapter of remarkable predictions which reveal God's complete sovereign control of all future history, confirming the absolute divine inspiration of all Scripture. Daniel's fourth and longest vision concerning his dear people's future has almost ended with the judgement of their greatest adversary. It remains for the angel to explain Israel's great and final deliverance in the first four verses of chapter 12, to which we now turn.

Understanding the End Times of Great Tribulation, Resurrection, and Millennial Blessing

Chapter 12 is the high point of the Book of Daniel and may be divided into three main sections: 1) *The Climax of Daniel's Fourth Vision*, verses 1-4; 2) *The Confirmation of the Duration of the Time of the End*, verses 5-8; 3) *The Concluding Explanations by the Angel to Daniel*, verses 9-13.

1. The Climax of Daniel's Fourth Vision, vv.1-4

These verses reveal that the time of the end has particular relevance to Daniel's people, Israel, who will then be fully and finally delivered from the persecutions of their enemies. Furthermore, that will be the time when the two resurrections and judgements will occur, and all will receive their due rewards of blessing for faithfulness to God or retribution for evil.

The whole section from chapter 11 verse 36 to chapter 12 verse 3 reveals the seven major features of the time of the end, which is still future to our own day, namely: 1) A world ruler; 2) A world religion; 3) A world war; 4) A great tribulation for Israel; 5) A great deliverance for Israel at its end; 6) Two resurrections; and 7) The ultimate reward of the righteous. From Daniel chapter 9 verses 26-27 we may also learn that the time of the end will begin when 'the prince that shall come' breaks his seven-year covenant of protection with Israel at the mid-point of that period. Daniel chapter 7 verse 25 has already indicated that this time will last for three and a half years, in line with other Scriptures such as Revelation 13 verse 5, and that it is to be identified with the time of Jacob's trouble (Jeremiah chapter 30 verse 7) and the Great Tribulation predicted by the Lord Jesus Himself in His Olivet Discourse (Matthew chapter 24 verse 21). It is fully described in Revelation chapters 6-19.

Verse 1: The Great Tribulation and Israel's Deliverance

The opening words of chapter 12, 'at that time', make it clear to us that this verse is referring to the same period as that described as 'the time of the end' in chapter 11 verse 40, the final great world war. At that time there will be an intervention in Israel's situation by the great archangel Michael, whose role is especially to defend the interests of Daniel's beloved people in the world, the Jews, as we have already seen in chapter 10. Revelation chapter 12 will further reveal to church saints that at that time Michael and his angels will wage war on Satan and his hosts in heaven and cast them out of that sphere on to the earth fully and finally. This will intensify the unprecedented troubles on earth already affecting the world during the first half of the seven-year Tribulation period.

We must also note that this time of tribulation will affect 'the children of thy (Daniel's) people', Israel, not the New Testament Church, which is promised exemption from 'the hour of trial that is to come upon the whole habitable world' in Revelation chapter 3 verse 10, and also in other similar New Testament Scriptures. In fact, the New Testament promises that the Church will be raptured to heaven by Christ at His Coming for them to the air (1 Thessalonians chapter 4 verses 13 to 18) and thus be delivered from the coming time of God's wrath against mankind (1 Thessalonians chapter 1 verses 9-10), since we are not appointed to face God's wrath at all, but to obtain salvation from it (1 Thessalonians chapter 5 verse 9). When all this is happening on the earth, we shall be with the Lord in His Father's house in heaven, according to the promise of the Lord Jesus to His own in the upper room (John chapter 14 verses 1-

3). Israel, by contrast with the Church, is God's earthly chosen people, not His heavenly people, and has a different role, place, and destiny in God's purposes for the world. We should not confuse the two, as Amillennial interpreters of Scripture do. Israel in Scripture always refers to the earthly people of God, while the Church always refers to His present heavenly people. In Acts chapter 7 verse 38 the reference by Stephen to 'the church in the wilderness' means 'the congregation of Israel in the wilderness', not the New Testament Church.

At all events, after enduring the most traumatic time of trouble they have ever endured, Israel will be delivered in a remarkable way, as other Scriptures confirm, by the personal intervention of Christ returning in power and glory to rule and to reign over the world for a thousand years; see Zechariah chapter 14 for this miraculous deliverance at the very moment when all will seem lost for the surviving Jews in Jerusalem. Zechariah chapter 13 also reveals that two-thirds of the nation will die in the final battle for the city, but that one third will survive and be converted in a day when they see Christ their Messiah coming to reign. This time of trouble will correspond to and be part of the great world war described in chapter 11 verses 40-45.

'Every one that shall be found written in the book' refers to those who have their names written in the book of life, otherwise called the Lamb's book of life; see Exodus 32.32-33; Psalm 69.28; Revelation 13.8; 17.8; 20.15; and 21.27. Not every individual Israelite will be ready for the coming of Christ, and some will have to be judged as rebels, according to Ezekiel chapter 20 verses 33-38; but Israel as a nation will be saved from their persecutors, according to Romans chapter 11 verse 26. This very passage in Daniel indicates that there will be two different groups of Israelites at the time of the end, the righteous and the wicked, and that they will have two different destinies. No Israelite who is not born again by faith in Christ will enter the millennial kingdom of God; see John chapter 3 verse 5.

Verse 2: the Two Resurrections of the Just and the Unjust

This verse reveals that at the end of the Tribulation, when Israel is fully and finally delivered from their enemies at the Second Coming of Christ, there will be a resurrection from the dead. Revelation chapter 20 further reveals that there will actually be two separate resurrections; first, that of believers, the righteous, before the millennial kingdom, followed a thousand years later after the end of that kingdom by that of all unbelievers, the unrighteous. The Lord Jesus Himself in John's Gospel chapter 5 also referred to the resurrection of the just and the unjust, implying a difference of some kind between the two. That difference is only hinted at here in Daniel, but can be inferred from the repetition of the word 'some', which is actually 'these' in the Hebrew. Now the righteous dead who will be resurrected at this point will probably include both the Old Testament believers and the Tribulation martyrs, but not the New Testament Church saints. 1 Thessalonians chapter 4 reveals by a further 'word of the Lord' that all Church believers who have died will be resurrected at the same time as the living Church saints are raptured to heaven, or rather, a fraction of a second before the latter are raptured, at the coming of the Lord to the air for them. The New Testament indicates that the Rapture of the Church will take place before the Tribulation ever begins; see Revelation chapter 3 verse 10; 1 Thessalonians chapter 1 verses 9-10; chapter 5 verse 9. And it is very unlikely that Old Testament believers will be resurrected at the same time as the Church saints, because the Church is separate from Israel and the Gentiles in God's purposes throughout Scripture, and is in many ways unique. In Ephesians and Colossians the Church is called a 'mystery' hidden in God throughout the Old Testament ages and generations, being the highest point in God's purposes of redemption, but not revealed to men before New Testament times. It is much more likely that Old Testament believers will be resurrected at the beginning of the millennial kingdom along with the Tribulation martyrs and will then enjoy millennial blessing.

Some commentators, however, including many of the older assembly writers and a few more recent assembly writers, have doubted that this verse does refer to physical resurrection. Instead, they hold that it refers to Israel's national spiritual revival. They compare this verse with Ezekiel chapter 37, the vision of the valley of dry bones, which certainly does refer to Israel's national spiritual awakening and restoration. They also think that Old Testament believers will be resurrected at the same time as the Church saints at the Rapture. Although no really major doctrinal issue is involved in this question, the present writer inclines to agree with the view of many of the more recent North American Premillennial commentators that physical resurrection, not just spiritual awakening and revival, is in view here. How else are we to understand the end of the verse, 'and some to shame and everlasting contempt', since this clearly refers to the final and eternal judgement of the unrighteous (unbelievers) at the Great White Throne judgement of Revelation chapter 20? Also, the argument of the uniqueness of the New Testament Church in God's dispensational purposes with mankind would support the view that its Resurrection and Rapture will not be shared with Old Testament saints, but be a quite separate event. Rather, this verse in Daniel would more naturally indicate that Old Testament saints will be resurrected at the same time as the Tribulation martyrs somewhat later than the Church saints, and that this resurrection will occur at the Second Coming of Christ right down to the earth to reign, not when He comes to the air. It has been helpfully observed that God's three great programmes for the world concern, first, the kingdom, secondly Israel, and thirdly the Church, in that order, but that He will complete these three great programmes in reverse order as to their historical fulfilment. In other words, first He will complete His programme for the Church, His heavenly people, secondly His programme for Israel, His earthly people, and lastly His programme for the kingdom. This observation would again support the priority and uniqueness of God's dealings with the Church, and confirm the view advocated here that Old

Testament saints will not be raptured at the same time as the Church, but after the Tribulation has taken place, and before the commencement of Christ's millennial kingdom.

Physical resurrection is taught in a few Old Testament Scriptures, although not very many. Abraham believed in resurrection when he offered up Isaac on Mount Moriah; see Genesis chapter 22 verse 5 and compare it with Hebrews chapter 11 verse 19. Job, who probably lived at about the same time as Abraham, or even earlier, also believed in physical resurrection; see Job chapter 19 verses 25-26. Isaiah, who lived about a century before Daniel, predicted in his prophecy chapter 26 verse 19 that dead men would live again and their bodies rise from the grave. Hosea, a contemporary of Isaiah, predicted in Hosea chapter 13 verse 14, 'I will ransom them from the power of the grave, I will redeem them from death'. The resurrection of Christ is predicted in Psalm 16 verses 9-10, as Peter confirms on the Day of Pentecost in Acts chapter 2. And both Elijah and Elisha were enabled to bring back to life again boys who had died. So this verse in Daniel would add to the Old Testament evidence for the doctrine of physical resurrection and reveal somewhat more about it than had been revealed up until that time, namely, the time of the resurrection of Old Testament saints. Also, it adds to the evidence for a number of separate resurrections in Scripture.

Verse 3: the Reward of the Righteous

Here we have explained the future reward of the righteous dead who will be raised to life again at this time. They are described as 'the wise', that is, those who feared the Lord, and as those who 'turn many to righteousness', having preached righteousness to their contemporaries and caused many of them to turn to God in repentance and faith. Their reward will be a place of further witness and glory in the coming kingdom of Christ on earth. They will be those who enjoy the 'everlasting life' spoken of in verse 2. Particularly in mind here in Daniel chapter 12 are probably those spoken of in chapter 11 verse 32, who 'know their God'. Verse 33 of that chapter had also said that 'they that understand among the people shall instruct many', and verse 35 had called them 'them of understanding'. This was fulfilled in the second century B.C. in the time of the Maccabean revolt from Antiochus Epiphanes. But it will equally apply to many others who have lived and died for God and His truth during all previous centuries, including the Tribulation period. How faithful and wise have we been in our own day of witness for God? For according to that will be our own reward in glory too.

Verse 4: the Conclusion of the Vision
Daniel's long fourth vision had now finished. The angel who communicated it to him instructed him to seal up the book containing the words of the vision which he had recorded, because it was not meant to be understood before the time of the end. This is by contrast with the instruction given by the risen Lord Jesus in Revelation chapter 22 verse 10 to the apostle John not to seal up his visions contained in that book, because the time was at hand for its fulfilment, that is, imminent to both his and our own day. But it does also mean that we today, because we live near to this 'time of the end', can expect to understand more about the prophecies contained in the Book of Daniel than any previous generation of believers so far have. This we find to be the case, although some detailed passages of the prophecies remain somewhat difficult to interpret with any degree of certainty. How privileged we are to live in these closing days of the Age of Grace before the end times really begin in earnest after the Rapture of the Church! How responsible we are, too, to warn the unsaved of their coming fate, if they do not repent, and to encourage our fellow-believers in our common faith and hope in Christ!

The second half of the verse probably does not refer so much to the modern increase in travel and the information explosion in the world generally at the time of the end, although that has also happened, as to diligent study of this Book of Daniel by believers and concerned unbelievers, and their consequent increased understanding of the book in the time of the end. 'Run to and fro' probably refers to reading the lines on a page of a book with the eyes. During the time of Tribulation many will investigate this prophecy of Daniel, learn from it the meaning of events transpiring around them, and so be guided by it in their lives at that time. How good God is to tell us so much about what lies ahead for this world as a whole, as well as about our own destiny! But it is intended to guide us in our relationship both with the world around us and with one another in the Body of Christ today. How diligent and circumspect we should be in our witness and behaviour in the world today, so near now to 'the time of the end'!

2. The Confirmation of the Duration of the Time of the End, vv.5-8

Daniel records that, after the angel had at last finished relating to him the details of his fourth and longest vision, he looked up and saw two figures standing one on either bank of the River Tigris. One of the figures, who is not identified, but was presumably an angel, spoke to the other figure, who is described as 'the man clothed in linen', whom we have met before in chapter 10 verses 5 and 6. He is therefore to be identified as a Theophany, probably the Lord Himself, the pre-incarnate Son of God. The angel asked the Lord how long it would be until the end of all these wonderful, but terrifying, revelations. The Lord, who was standing by the river waters, held up both His hands to heaven and swore an oath by the Eternal God that the end of the vision's events would come after 'a time, times, and half a time', as is predicted in chapter 7 verse 25, that is, after three and a half years. As we have previously explained, this corresponds to the second half of the seven-year period mentioned in chapter 9 verse 27. During this limited, but terrible, period of intense tribulation God will allow the Man of Sin, the first Beast of Revelation chapter 13, to shatter the strength of His holy people, Israel, but after that their trials will at last end. Daniel, concerned as he was to hear about his beloved people Israel's welfare, could not take in this revelation, and so simply asked again what the end of all these things was going to be. Would not Israel have suffered enough by this time? How and when, then, would all their sufferings ever end? Daniel, like all the Old Testament prophets, was a true patriot, although fully aware of his beloved people's great and many sins, and longed to hear of future blessing for them. Are we today at all like him? How much do we love the people around us in the world and how much do we love our fellow-brethren and sisters in the assembly, in spite of all their faults?

3. The Concluding Explanations by the Angel to Daniel, vv.9-13

In this concluding paragraph of the book the angel only partially answers Daniel's question in verse 8. God does not always answer all our questions about the future or other matters, but just sufficient of them to promote our spiritual good; for He must remain transcendent God in His own creation. So Daniel was here told, rather abruptly, to go his way, that is, that he would soon die and be gathered to his fathers. It was not for him to know the full meaning of all that he had seen in his visions; that was intended to remain a closed and sealed book until the fulfilment was near at the time of the end of Gentile rule over the world. Now the angel explains that the events of this time of the end will have a two-fold effect on mankind as a whole. On the one hand, many who respond to them in repentance and faith will be purified by all their sufferings for Christ's sake in those days of trial and tribulation. On the other hand, the unrepentant wicked majority of men will only become more hardened in heart by them, and will continue in all their wicked ways. Because they have rejected all God's overtures of love and grace towards them, the wicked will become unable to understand the true meaning of the end time events unfolding before their very eyes; but the wise, that is, believers who fear God and live righteous lives before Him, will be able from these Scriptures to understand their import clearly and so to respond accordingly. In this way these prophecies will prove to be very practical in their effect. We should note here that it will be impossible in those days for anyone to remain neutral in his or her allegiance and response to divine revelation. Either, they will become wise, that is, saved believers, or they will be confirmed in their natural wickedness and unbelief, and so be lost and condemned at the judgement.

Now at the end of the book the angel does give some further revelations concerning the duration of the time of the end, as Daniel had requested of him, and adds a few facts concerning the time needed to prepare the world for the millennial rule of Christ. He links these further revelations with the starting-point of the events of the Great Tribulation as previously predicted in chapter 9 verse 27. There Gabriel had predicted that the time of tribulation would begin when 'the prince that should come', the first Beast of Revelation chapter 13, stopped the Jews offering their daily sacrifices according to the Levitical law, so breaking his seven-year covenant of protection with them, and set up his own image in the rebuilt temple in Jerusalem as the object of universal worship, which image is called the 'abomination of desolation' by the Lord Jesus Himself in Matthew chapter 24 verse 15. The reference clearly goes quite beyond what Antiochus Epiphanes would do earlier during his occupation of Jerusalem, and relates to the end time events. After that event there will be two different, though related, periods of days to be reckoned before the kingdom of Christ will be fully set up. The Great Tribulation will last 1260 days according to the Book of Revelation, or three and a half years. But here we learn that the blessings of the kingdom will not be experienced until 1290 days have elapsed. And even that time will not be sufficient for everything to happen as predicted in various prophecies. The full blessing will not come before 1335 days have passed. Now what may be the significance of these two additional periods added to the length of the Tribulation? We suggest that the 1290 and 1335 days will perhaps be necessary for Christ, after His coming to earth, to defeat all His enemies in the nations around Israel, such as Edom, according to Isaiah chapter 63, and to conduct the judgement of the living nations, according to Matthew chapter 25 verses 31-46, and the judgement of Israel in the wilderness, according to Ezekiel chapter 20 verses 34-38. Some time will be needed to complete all these judgements. Also, the earth will need to be restored after the devastating judgements of the Tribulation in readiness for the commencement of the reign of Christ over the world in peace and righteousness. These extra days, therefore, will probably be days of final preparation for the setting up of the millennial kingdom. Those who attain to the end of those days are described as blessed, because they have proved by their allegiance to Christ, the King, that they are worthy to enter the kingdom.

The angel finishes his prophecies to the aged prophet by confirming that Daniel is soon to depart this life, to die and rest in peace from all his earthly labours until the time of the end of which he has been speaking. But he also promises that then Daniel will stand in his lot at the end of the days mentioned just previously. This is a prediction of Daniel's physical resurrection, along with all Old Testament saints, after the end of the Tribulation to enjoy the blessings of Christ's kingdom. It also reveals that Daniel will have a special 'lot', or role, in the administration of that kingdom, as indeed Scripture indicates that some other Old Testament saints will have. Incidentally, this final prediction would tend to confirm the view expressed above that the Old Testament saints will not be resurrected with the Church saints at the Rapture of the Church, but will have to wait until after the Tribulation has ended; for what will be true of Daniel must be true of all such saints.

We do not know exactly when Daniel died, but it must have been a little after he had seen this long vision in 536 B.C. in the third year of Cyrus. He would have needed some further time to write his book as we have it today, although perhaps not a very long time after that date. At all events, Daniel must have lived at least until he was nearly ninety years old. God often does grant His most faithful servants a long and productive life on earth, although that is not always true. Daniel, however, is three times in his book called 'a man greatly-beloved', and God certainly favoured him as His specially-chosen vessel to accomplish a unique task for Himself in this world. May each one of us seek in our own day and circle of witness to live for God's glory as faithfully as Daniel did!

CHAPTER 13

Daniel's Spiritual Legacy
for Believers Today

As Christian believers, we all face the searching review and rigorous assessment of our personal lives, characters, and service for our Lord at the Judgement Seat of Christ following our Rapture to heaven. But also, consider that, if we die before the Lord comes again, we shall inevitably leave behind us a spiritual legacy for other believers who will live after we have departed this life. It is a serious thought to consider just what kind of spiritual good we are likely to leave behind us for others to benefit from. The writer to the Hebrew Christians, in chapter 13 of his letter to them, certainly encouraged his readers to consider the spiritual legacy which their now departed leaders had left them, with a view to following and imitating their good example of faith. Now when we consider the spiritual legacy which God's greatly-beloved servant Daniel has left us in the record of his life, service, and prophecies, there is very much from which we can benefit today. We shall therefore consider his spiritual legacy under four separate headings, as follows:-

1. His Exemplary Personal Conduct
No particular sin or misdemeanour is recorded in connection with Daniel's personal life and conduct. He was utterly faithful to God and His Word even in the face of acute danger. Like us, Daniel was a sinner by nature, but his recorded life is one free from any significant blemishes. He was loyal to his friends, wise

and kind to his enemies, and patriotic towards his captive people, Israel. His whole life was governed by his reverential fear of the Lord his God. Is ours?

2. His Irreproachable Public Service
Daniel served with distinction and complete integrity in the highest echelons of the administrations of most of the Babylonian monarchs and the earliest of the Persian kings. Nebuchadnezzar was so influenced by him that he was eventually converted, while Darius the Mede made him his right-hand man. His enemies could find nothing against him in his handling of the affairs of the kingdom. Could the same be said of us in our various secular relationships and responsibilities?

3. His Consistent and Effective Prayer Life
Daniel is still known today as a great man of prayer. His regular habit was to pray three times daily, as well as at other times, regardless of who was observing him. His fervent prayers for his people Israel were largely instrumental in effecting their restoration to their Promised Land at the end of the Babylonian Exile. God always heard his prayers, although the answers to them were sometimes delayed by evil angelic opposition. So close a relationship did he constantly enjoy with his God. He was certainly an example of a righteous man whose prayers were always earnest and prevailed with God. Are ours?

4. His Panoramic Prophecies concerning the Times of the Gentiles
God revealed to Daniel probably more concerning the future of both Gentile and Jewish history than to any other Old Testament prophet. The prophecies in his book span the entire period of Gentile rule in the world during the so-called 'Times of the Gentiles', from 605 B.C. until the Second Coming of Christ. He was used by God to present us with an unparalleled and breathtaking panorama of world history, both now past and also future to us. No other Old Testament prophecy is so

comprehensive in its scope or so detailed in its presentation. And the future of Israel under Gentile dominion is here outlined in great detail, too, right up to their final deliverance from oppression at the Second Coming and millennial kingdom of Christ. Truly, Daniel was a chosen vessel in God's sovereign overruling hand to reveal His purposes of judgement and grace in the world for at least two and a half millennia of years from his own day. Few other men have enjoyed such a privileged role in God's dealings with mankind. Today we simply marvel as we continue to see his prophecies coming true in human history around us. Surely, this causes us, as members of the New Testament Church, to lift up our heads in anticipation of our Lord's return to the air for His own blood-bought heavenly people, and to cry meaningfully, 'Even so, come, Lord Jesus!'

A Final Challenge

In the light of such a wonderful spiritual legacy as Daniel the statesman and prophet of the Lord has left us, we should be exercised to cultivate similar traits of godly character, even though we may never be granted his exceptional abilities or gifts, nor have such great opportunities to use them in our Lord's service. Like Daniel, we are all greatly loved by God, and may enjoy a similar fellowship with Him to that which Daniel enjoyed. In particular, we today are privileged to live in the lengthening shadows of the end times, and can clearly see around us events which will fulfil the prophecies given to Daniel to record, but which he himself was never able fully to understand. In that respect we are even more highly-favoured than Daniel was. We are therefore more responsible than he was to live in the light of the many Scriptures which are about to be fulfilled. Let us make it our one aim to please the Lord who died to save us from the coming judgements, and to cultivate an ever closer relationship with the Most High God of heaven who has condescended to make us His own and to include us in His confidence and plans for eternity!